Ancient Britons and the Antiquarian Imagination

STUART PIGGOTT

Ancient Britons and the Antiquarian Imagination

Ideas from the Renaissance to the Regency

WITH 50 ILLUSTRATIONS

THAMES AND HUDSON

*To the Memory of Glyn Daniel in
Friendship and Gratitude*

Printed in the German Democratic Republic by Interdruck

Contents

Preface

It is now just a half-century ago that I first published an essay on antiquarian history in Britain, and since then the subject has continued to interest and fascinate me. In 1950 I published my biography of William Stukeley and simultaneously Sir Thomas Kendrick his *British Antiquity*. Then and later he urged me to take up the story of British antiquarianism where he had ended his brilliant study, approximately with William Camden, and encouraged and helped me in the various short essays I published in his lifetime. In expressing my gratitude to his memory it is also appropriate to put on record my early debt to those two friends and mentors in biography and history, Lord David Cecil and Mr G.M. Young.

Many have helped me in writing the present book and I would like to thank particularly Dr Iain Brown, Professor J.M. Levine and Dr Elaine Paintin. The staff of Thames and Hudson have as usual given me every help and support. In planning the book and in its early stages I was encouraged, aided and cheered by Glyn Daniel, whose untimely death cut short a close friendship of long standing. He would have read and criticized my drafts, a task taken on by his widow: Ruth Daniel's sound critical judgment has meant much in writing the present text. As a personal tribute I have dedicated this book to Glyn Daniel's memory.

West Challow, October 1988

Introduction – the search for ancient Britain

This book sets out to give an account of how British scholars, from the Renaissance to the Regency, sought to construct a picture of their remote ancestors before the Roman conquest. We would now call this period 'prehistoric', but the word was only coined to express a then novel concept in 1851 by Daniel Wilson in his *Prehistoric Annals of Scotland*, and came into general use with the publication in 1865 of Sir John Lubbock's *Prehistoric Times*. For the antiquaries, and indeed the whole literate public over the period with which we will be concerned, the word would be meaningless, for the Universe was entirely historical from its Creation, documented in an infallible text by an unimpeachable author, the Old Testament recording God's word. History began with the first chapter of the Book of Genesis.

If the field of study was not thought of as 'prehistoric', nor was the means used to investigate it recognized as 'archaeology'. The word was sometimes used, from the early seventeenth century, to denote the study of the past and of antiquities, and in the period with which we are directly concerned it was used by two writers in the 1720s, Henry Rowlands and Alexander Gordon, in the restricted sense of being concerned with monuments rather than documents, but they are exceptional. In the event, the most significant advances in the comprehension of antiquity, leading to what we distinguish as archaeology, were made as a result of the Intellectual Revolution of the later seventeenth century, when as a part of a more widespread inductive approach to natural and artificial phenomena characterized by the early Royal Society, the material evidence of early man, such as field monuments like stone circles or small artifacts like flint implements, came to be described and classified in terms which would now be called archaeological.

It would then be misleading to regard the present essay as in some way a chapter in a 'History of Archaeology'. One cannot see archaeology emerging as a recognizable discipline until the later nineteenth century; before this we have an amorphous antiquarianism. So-called histories of archaeology almost invariably, despite their titles, devote themselves exclusively to prehistoric archaeology. This is indefensible: for the restricted area of Britain, for instance, a history of archaeology, after prehistory, must engage in the archaeological evidence for the Roman occupation, with the increased complexity of not only military and civil field monuments and material culture in the technology of artifacts, but of numismatics and epigraphy and the specialized archaeology that constitutes art history. In the post-Roman and early Middle Ages, archaeology technically indistinguishable from that employed for prehistory at first predominates, soon to be aided by documentary evidence and increasingly the collateral archaeology of coins, art and architectural history[1] added to the study of technology. All this is archaeology, and to the early antiquaries there were no distinctions made, largely because the evidence was not available or recognized as such. Much of the material culture of Roman Britain was seen as such from the Renaissance, but Sir Thomas Browne could regard his pagan Saxon pottery from Old Walsingham as Roman; the recognition of Anglo-Saxon archaeology only dates from James Douglas (1752–1819).

What is offered here is an enquiry into the idea of early British antiquity as it became an object of interest among the scholars who called themselves antiquaries from the late sixteenth century to the first decade of the nineteenth. This interest was at times considerable, at others negligible. Historians of the natural sciences, which in some respects offer parallels to archaeology, have made the point that it is a cardinal fallacy to regard their early stages as 'a progressive struggle of enlightened intellects to free human knowledge from the shackles of obscurantist attitudes', where from a modern viewpoint one issues judgments on 'those who have been "correct" and those whose opinions have been "erroneous".' Rather we should try to see them as 'men of their own time, grappling with problems which they rarely had enough evidence to solve, and solving them, if at all, in terms of their own views of the world.'[2] In our own study, Dr Plot in 1686 may receive modern approbation for recording the ring-ditches in the meadows of North Oxford, but we must remember that he thought that though some might be caused by witches (in which he believed) dancing in fairy-rings at their Sabbaths, the majority were the result of bolts of lightning striking the earth. And a couple of years before in Scotland Sir Robert Sibbald certainly described and illustrated prehistoric flint arrowheads, but firmly believed they were elf-bolts shot from the heavens or by fairies and witches. We have to see the early antiquaries in terms of their own world-pictures and not anachronistically transfer them to our own.

With these preliminaries, we may turn to the plan of the present book. In the first chapter, the Antiquary as a recognizable character is introduced, with his origins in the Italian Renaissance and its rediscovery of the classical past in antiquities as well as in texts. In Britain we see, largely it must be admitted in humorous caricature, the emergence and establishment in the seventeenth century of the student of antiquities as a type in the world of learning and in a form which was to continue into the nineteenth century. The main antiquarian figures who contributed to the study of pre-Roman Britain, and not those whose interests lay elsewhere, are then introduced to the reader so that when their ideas come to be discussed in subsequent chapters they will not be wholly unfamiliar personalities. The ancient Briton was to be pursued by individuals, few if any of whom were consciously trying to build on or improve upon the work of their predecessors; there is no sense of an emergent and developing tradition. In the early decades of the Royal Society one is keenly aware of its deliberate fostering of what is from the first recognizable as something new, that would become the scientific tradition, but the Society of Antiquaries, founded in 1717, at no time from then until the nineteenth century gives any impression of being aware of the new potentialities of archaeology rather than of old-fashioned antiquarianism. The story is then one of individuals without the intellectual support of an institution, and the Society figures little in subsequent pages.

An aspect of the study of ancient man, too often in the past ignored or dismissed as tiresomely irrelevant, is that of the profound influence, in all early thought of antiquity, of the Biblical narrative of the Old Testament and particularly that of the Book of Genesis. The early antiquaries and their readers in Britain were all Christians, and almost all members of the Church of England, happily accommodated within its wide range of tolerated belief after the Restoration: even when John Toland, the Deist and writer on Druids and their stone circles, published his shocking pamphlet in 1696 its title was *Christianity Not Mysterious*, not 'Christianity Non-Existent'. The Bible took its place as an authoritative text at a time when the writers of antiquity were the unquestioned source of information on the past, and as such deeply coloured the conceptual world of the antiquaries. The second chapter is concerned with this influence of the Bible and other texts of real or imagined antiquity from the Creation to the Flood; the third begins with the question, directly of concern to the students of the earliest inhabitants of Britain, of the part played by the descendants of Noah in the peopling of the west. It continues with the estimates made of the cultural status of immediately post-Diluvial man in Britain, and how these were further moulded by the references to Britain in the classical texts from Caesar and Tacitus to Dio and Herodian and by the ethnographic parallels which were drawn from Britain and, over-whelmingly important, from the newly discovered American Indians.

By the late seventeenth century a picture of the ancient Briton as a painted, skin-clad savage was formed and the fourth chapter sets out the problems encountered by the early antiquaries in the recognition of prehistoric artifacts first of stone and then of bronze. Stone and flint tools had to be recognized as artificial and not natural: once they could be attributed to Caesar's more barbarous aborigines bronze-working seemed a sophistication incompatible with such savagery, and a Roman origin for prehistoric bronzes more probable. The first field monuments to be claimed for the pre-Roman Britons were the megaliths and stone circles, where John Aubrey and Edward Lhuyd made their classic contributions; in the absence of excavation barrows remained enigmatic, and earthworks insoluble mysteries. The last chapter shows how this state of knowledge was hardly advanced in the eighteenth century, and though William Stukeley set new standards of detailed record in the field at Avebury and Stonehenge, in his early years he was a belated Restoration antiquary and in his later invented and propagated romantic nonsense on the Druids that unfortunately had a disastrous popularity with a credulous public in a time of decline in scholarly standards. Theoretical schemes of man's early develop-ment, grandiose in sweep but innocent of archaeology, became popular with the philosophers and attractive to the literary world. At the very end of the century a new wealth of empirical evidence was suddenly available with the barrow digging of William Cunnington and Sir Richard Colt Hoare on the Wiltshire downs, but the techniques of excavation were as primitive as those of Sir Thomas Browne's day and the conceptual framework within the evidence could be under-stood as that of Aubrey.

This long record of irregular achievement and failure may be somewhat different from that of the continuous and inevitable, if slow, progress in the foundation of archaeology that is sometimes assumed, but it is a pattern imposed by the evidence. The views of the antiquaries have where possible been presented by quotations at length from their own writings, for these not only convey their difficulties and underlying habits of thought, but in their prose indicate something of their characters. The charming diffidence of John Aubrey's scholarship is as apparent in the style of the *Monumenta Britannica* as in his *Brief Lives*: his remark in the latter, 'How these curiosities would be quite forgott, did not such idle fellowes as I am putt them down!' might equally apply to both. The profuse italics and capitals of Robert Plot betray the pomposity of the writer, and the brisk liveliness of William Stukeley's writing in the 1720s contrasts with the flabby vagueness of his effusions on the Druids in later years. It is as individuals, sometimes eccentric, that they made their contribution to knowledge, and as such they should be understood and remembered.

When we come to assess the contribution made by the antiquaries between about 1580 and 1800 to what later became the discipline of prehistoric archaeology, one phenomenon immediately stands out, the achievement of the late seventeenth century. An historian, Professor Pat Rogers, has very recently and in a wider context written of 'Gibson's edition of Camden's *Britannia*, one of the key works in the formation of the eighteenth-century mind'[3] and this perceptive estimate is welcome. In our restricted field, the 1695 Camden is the standard of excellence against all that went before and came after must be judged, the *Britannia* not only of Camden but of Aubrey and Lhuyd and its brilliant young editors Gibson and Tanner. It represents a peak of achievement, a vigorous statement of new scholarship, a text to which the eighteenth century at best added footnotes. Of this achievement, its main contribution to subsequent archaeology was the establishment of the inductive discipline of inference from material culture, whether in the field or the museum, as an intellectual tool in elucidating the past.

For the world in general, the legacy of the early antiquaries has been an ambiguous one. It was they who, as a part of a pessimistic view of the first inhabitants of Britain, fallen from grace so far from Eden, created the stereotype of the brutish, skin-clad, club-bearing hunter that was to flourish in popular imagination down to the present day, now silted down into the world of children's comics with The Flintstones and Stonehenge Kit The Ancient Brit. On the other hand eighteenth-century romanticism and above all William Stukeley invented the Druids as a component of the myth of the Noble Savage. They drifted away from archaeology and the world of reason to find a home among those seeking an optimistic picture of ancient wisdom and prehistoric sages, even today finding acceptance among, in Sir Peter Medawar's words, that 'large population of people, often with well-developed literary and scholarly tastes, who have been educated far beyond their capacity to undertake analytical thought'.[4]

Eighteenth-century thinking about ancient man and the evolution of his social structure, not by antiquaries but by theoretical philosophers, was to have a far more serious outcome. The late eighteenth-century 'Conjectural History', as a contemporary styled it, set up a hypothetical sequence from savagery to civilization, and it was popularized by, among others, Rousseau; by 1877 an American, Lewis Morgan, produced an elaborated version based on his reading of American Indian anthropology. This much impressed Karl Marx and was even more enthusiastically taken up by Friedrich Engels, so that the speculations of the Scottish and French philosophers of the Enlightenment, quite unconnected with archaeology, have become a part of Marxist conjectural history today.[5]

And the eighteenth-century concept of the ancient Briton finds expression in unexpected contexts. Probably few archaeologists today, as they approach the British Museum, even if they do glance at Sir Robert Smirke's noble façade, have ever considered the sculpture in the pediment, executed by Sir Richard Westmacott in 1842–4. As his own description tells us, it depicts The Progress of Civilization, and 'commencing at the Eastern end . . . man is represented as emerging from a rude savage state, through the influence of religion. He is next personified as a hunter, and a tiller of the earth . . . Patriarchal simplicity then becomes invaded and the worship of the true God defiled . . . Paganism prevails . . . Civilization is now presumed to have made considerable progress.'[6]

I

The British antiquaries

Renaissance humanism, in its Italian homeland from the fourteenth century onwards, was as much concerned with the rediscovery of Greek and Latin literature from newly found or newly understood manuscripts as it was with recovering knowledge of the antique past from inscriptions, coins, sculpture and architecture. The two branches of nascent scholarship were interdependent paths to the discovery of classical antiquity, and those concerned with *antiquitates* saw themselves, proudly and consciously, as the heirs of the ancients' curiosity about their own past, and especially Varro, writing in the mid-first century BC his *Antiquitates rerum humanorum et divinarum*. The wider classical usage was the first and more usual meaning of *antiquitates*, but by 1527 Andrea Fulvio was using it in its modern sense of 'antiquities' in his *Antiquitates urbis*; before that, however, Flavio Biondo (1392–1463) in his great *Roma instaurata* of 1440–46 had demonstrated the potential independence of the antiquarian discipline. If he was the greatest exponent of the new antiquarianism he was by no means alone; one thinks of the visual records of Greek antiquities made by Cyriac of Ancona from 1423, and the new name gaining currency for such investigators of the non-literary sources for antiquity is given expression in Felice Feliciano (1433–80), who was known as *Antiquario*, the antiquary, from his (largely epigraphic) researches. By the end of the fifteenth century, the antiquary, recognized and named as such, was an acknowledged and respected figure among the humanists.[1]

All this is well known and has been admirably studied. It is a necessary preface to our immediate concern, the emergence in early modern Britain of students of the ancient past who were soon to be recognized, from the later sixteenth century at least, individually or corporately, as antiquaries by name. For it is among such scholars that the first tentative investigations into Britain's prehistoric past were made, which were to lead, often hesitantly, never consciously pursued as a coherent aim, to what became in the mid-nineteenth century the recognizable discipline of prehistoric archaeology. The early antiquaries in Britain were a very mixed crowd of genuine scholars, devoted pedants, ineffective triflers, credulous collectors and sheer crazy eccentrics, and by no means all were concerned with the evidence of surviving material culture or of Roman or pre-Roman antiquity; very many were minor documentary historians in such fields as legal history or genealogy, almost all seemed to have formed collections of antiquities of the most miscellaneous kind. But it was as antiquaries they were all known, among themselves and to the world at large.[2]

Probably the first to claim the title in England was the antiquarian topographer John Leland (*c.* 1503–1532), whose education included not only the universities of Cambridge and Oxford, but some years in Paris, where he came to know the Greek scholar and numismatist Guillaume Budé (1476–1540). Leland, to whom King Henry VIII granted a commission in 1533 'to peruse and diligently to serche al the libraries and collegies of this yowre noble reaulme', was consciously part of European humanism and knew where he stood in that world. Dedicating the first fruits of his topographical studies as a *Newe Yeares Gyfte* to the King in 1546 he ended proudly *Johannes Leylandus Antiquarius scripsit.* The title took root and Grafton in his *Chronicle* of 1563 refers as a matter of course to 'the booke of the excellent antiquary John Leyland', just as in 1602 we find the term with even more cause applied to 'our learned and studious Antiquarie Master Camden', whose justly famous *Britannia* had come out in 1586. In this year too it seems that a group of scholars in London formed themselves into a Society of Antiquaries which met for the reading of short papers and continued until 1614 when it was already in decline. King James I, it was reported, 'took a little Mislike' to the Society, suspecting it quite unjustly to have political overtones, and it came to an end. Its composition was largely legal and centred on the Inns of Court, though William Camden, then a master at Westminster School, and his friend and former pupil Sir Robert Bruce Cotton, were both members.

Antiquaries ridiculed

By the end of the sixteenth century the Antiquary was being recognized as a member of the English world of learning, as a distinctive character, and, alas, almost invariably as a figure of fun. But ridicule of an individual or a group indicates recognition within a society, and to be a target for wit acknowledges a common subject in everyday conversation sufficiently familiar to ensure that the point of the jest is seen. Antiquaries were worth laughing at as everyday members of English society, like parsons or lawyers. The note is set by Thomas Nashe in his *Pierce Penilesse* of 1592.

> An antiquary is an honest man, for he had rather scrape a piece of copper out of the dirt, than a crown from Ployden's standish [Edmund Plowden (1518–85) was a famous jurist, and the reference must be to taking a lawyer's fee]. I know many wise gentlemen of this musty vocation . . . A thousand gewgaws and toys have they in their chambers, which they heap up together, with infinite expense . . . This is the disease of our new-fangled humorists, they know not what to do with their wealth. It argueth a very rusty wit, so to doat on a wormeaten Eld.

There is a hint here of the legal antiquarians of the Elizabethan Society just mentioned, and the joke is at the expense of the clutter of useless antique objects with which they crowded their rooms and for which they paid ludicrous prices. At much the same time as Nashe, John Donne, then in his mid 20s, was making much the same kind of jest in his epigram on *Antiquary*, not published until 1633 –

> If in his Studie he hath so much care
> T'hang all old strange things, let his wife beware

and in his third *Satyre* (c. 1594–97) he enumerates marvels

> Stranger than seaven Antiquaries studies
> Than Africks Monsters, Guianaes rarities.

The antiquary's study, with its confusion of bric-a-brac and rusty knick-knacks, so deliciously to be described by Scott in *The Antiquary* of 1816, was clearly an established, and indeed one would have thought a rather tired stage set for comedy, two and a half centuries before Sir Walter's novel.

No foible or folly was likely to have been missed by the author of *The Anatomy of Melancholy*, and when in 1621 Robert Burton addresses us as 'Democritus to the Reader' we are hardly surprised to find him enumerating how

> Your supercilious Criticks, Grammatical triflers, Notemakers, curious Antiquaries, find out all the ruines of wit, *ineptiarum delicias*, amongst the rubbish of the old writers . . . puzzle themselves to find out how many streets in *Rome*, houses, gates, towers, *Homers* Countrey, *Aeneas* mother . . . what clothes the senators did wear in *Rome* . . . how they sate, where they went to the close-stool . . . is to them precious elaborate stuff . . .

Here for once we are spared the cabinet of curiosities, and the ridicule is instead directed at the very nature of antiquarian studies – the topography of ancient Rome, so devotedly explored by Flavio Biondo and his colleagues, the domestic manners and customs of antiquity – all trifles beside the majestic story of the heroes of Greece and Rome, who provided the matter of real history, history as moral philosophy teaching by example. And here we touch on what was to emerge on a far wider intellectual front as the Battle of the Ancients and Moderns.

The best known piece of ridicule of the seventeenth-century antiquary was to be published only seven years after Burton, when 'An Antiquary' was included in John Earle's *Micro-cosmographie or a Piece of the World discovered in Essayes and Characters* of 1628. Earle, who was to become Bishop of Salisbury, published this delightfully high-spirited *jeu d'esprit* when still in his 20s at Oxford, and his book was one of the earliest of many in seventeenth-century England based on the classical model of Theophrastus (about 300 BC); the Greek philosopher sketched thirty characters, Earle no less than seventy-eight, of which the Antiquary is no 9.

He is a man strangely thrifty of Time past, and an enemy indeed to his Maw, whence he fetches out many things when they are now all rotten and stinking. Hee is one that hath that unnatural disease to bee enamour'd of old age and wrinckles, and loves all things (as Dutchmen doe Cheese) the better for being mouldy and worme-eaten . . . A great admirer is he of the rust of old Monuments . . . Hee will goe you forty miles to see a *Saints Well* or a ruin'd Abbey . . . His estate consists much in shekels, and Roman Coynes . . . Beggars coozen him with musty things they have rak'd from dunghills . . . His chamber is commonly hung with strange Beasts skins, and is a kinde of Charnel-house of bones extraordinary . . . His grave do's not frighten him, for he ha's bene us'd to Sepulchers, and he likes Death the better, because it gathers him to his Fathers.

Comic but affectionate, Earle's sketch neatly summed up the educated Englishman's estimate of antiquarian studies in his time, and set them into a perhaps rather unfortunate mould that would endure for over two centuries, though it must be admitted that many minor antiquaries over this time did more to perpetuate than to dispel the image.

It was inevitable, in a literary world of active playwrights, that the character should now appear on stage. A minor dramatist, Shackerley Marmion, came out in 1641 with a comedy, *The Antiquary*, with the part of 'Veterano the Antiquary' in its cast. It is a tedious farce, set inconsistently in Venice and Pisa, which is immaterial, since its characters are obviously English. Veterano is an old fool, based on Earle (a phrase of his is actually used at one point), though he does offer a defence of antiquities – 'they are the registers, the chronicles of the age they were made in, and speak the truth of history better than a hundred of your printed commentaries'. But he is the credulous collector of absurd bogus antiquities which crowd his house, 'rarities, such as the world cannot produce the like, snatch'd from the jaws of time'. The Long Parliament was to close the play-houses in 1642, but Marmion's play was to be resurrected three quarters of a century later, as we shall see. In the meantime the antiquary, surprisingly enough, enters the rogues' underworld, for 'B.E.Gent' included an entry in his *New Dictionary of the Terms Ancient and Modern of the Canting Crew. In its several TRIBES of Gypsies, Beggers, Thieves Cheats, &c* (1690)

Antiquary, a curious Critick in old Coins, Stones and Inscriptions, in Worm-eaten Records, and ancient Manuscripts; also one that affects and blindly doats, on Relicks, Ruins, old Customs, Phrases and Fashions.

One might have thought the jest to have run its course with the century, but it was not to be. We shall later deal with the serious intellectual debate between the humanities and the sciences, in the Battle of the Ancient and Moderns, the Virtuosi and the Wits, and in France until well into the eighteenth century, the acrimony between *les érudits* and *les philosophes*. Here ridicule played a large part, with antiquarian studies, despite their ostensible subject-matter of antiquity, sharing the odium of the modern sciences. At the beginning of the eighteenth century, in 1717, John Gay on behalf of the Wits, helped by Pope and Arbuthnot, decided to lampoon an identifiable Virtuoso, and in the farce *Three Hours After Marriage* Dr Fossile, a ludicrous figure of vanity, fantasy and imminent cuckoldry, is none other than Dr John Woodward, cosmologist, geologist and antiquary (and eventually founder of the Woodwardian Chair of Geology in the University of Cambridge).[3] The play, put on in January 1717, was a wild success – 'For five Days together, the Talk of the Town' – and it can hardly be coincidence that the same month saw the formal foundation of the Society of Antiquaries of London, replacing that which had, as we saw, existed between 1586 and 1614, and continuing uninterrupted until today. It can be no chance either that Marmion's old play was revived for a two nights' run in 1718. The decline after about 1730, not only of many branches of the natural sciences, such as those to become geomorphology and palaeontology, but of the discipline of history itself, will be discussed later, but for the present we must note that antiquarian studies followed the same melancholy pattern of decay. When the Society of Antiquaries was corporately ridiculed in 1776 by Samuel Foote's comedy *The Nabob*, where Act III opens with a meeting of the 'Antiquarian Society' and all the old jokes, themselves by now cobwebbed antiques, are once again brought out, one cannot but feel that the play comes all too close to the futile reality of antiquarian studies at the time, and to their formal representative body.[4] After this the mockery goes on, now almost mechanically, into the nineteenth century, with comic verses by William Combe on *Dr Syntax* (1812), and *Dr Prosody* (1821); the caricatures of Grose, Rowlandson and others, and a weary plethora of cracked chamber-pots masquerading as Boadicea's Night Urn.

Antiquaries on the defensive

For their part, the antiquaries cannot have been unaware of their sometimes rather ambiguous position in a world of learning in which their studies were still a novelty. John Aubrey put a significant point of time as late as the mid-seventeenth century – 'Till about the year 1649, 'twas held a strange presumption for a man to attempt an innovation in learning; and not to be good manners to be more knowing than his neighbours and forefathers' – but as we have seen antiquarian studies were establishing themselves in England a century earlier; Camden's *Britannia* of 1586, and the simultaneous foundation of the Elizabethan Society of Antiquaries, represent the flowering of a tradition already well formed. William Camden[5] himself, deliberately introducing the topographical antiquarian approach from Renaissance Italy, at the instance and encouragement of the international figure of the New Geography, Abraham Ortelius, tells us in his Preface how Ortelius 'did very earnestly sollicit me to acquaint the World with *Britain*, that ancient Island; that is, to restore Britain to its antiquities, and its Antiquities to Britain, to renew the memory of what was old, illustrate what was obscure, and settle what was doubtful.' He then proceeds to a modest but dignified defence of his enterprise, anticipating the critics. 'Yet', he goes on, 'as the difficulty of the design discourag'd me on the one side, so the honour of my native Country encourag'd me on the other; insomuch, that whilst I dreaded the task, yet could not decline doing what I was able for the Glory of my Country.' As a pioneer he knew he would be subject to criticism: 'Yet possibly I may seem guilty of imprudence, who though but a smatterer in the business of Antiquities, have appear'd a scribler upon the stage of this learned age, expos'd to the censures of wise and judicious men.' This was just a conventional pretence of diffidence – Camden knew perfectly well he was no smatterer or scribbler – and he ends his preface on the defensive

> Some there are who cry down the study of Antiquity with much contempt, as too curious a search after what is past; whose authority I shall not altogether slight, so shall I not much regard their judgment . . . if they not approve, at least, I hope [they] will pardon what I have attempted out of that zealous affection I profess for my Native Country.

These closing words of Camden's preface strike a key-note in the mood and temper of the age, the exuberant patriotism of a little post-medieval nation state newly conscious of its European position. Camden himself elsewhere in his *Britannia* gives exquisite expression to his feeling when he writes of Britain that

> It is the master-piece of Nature perform'd when she was in her best and gayest humour; which she placed as a little world by its self, by the side of the greater, for the diversion of mankind.

Contemporary literature reflects, and itself created and maintained the theme, and the antiquaries happily joined in. One of the founder members of the Elizabethan Society of Antiquaries, Arthur Agarde, Deputy-Chamberlain at the Exchequer, in a paper communicated in 1604 to the Society 'On the Diversity of Names of this Island' suddenly burst out

> And surely that sweet name of England hath been of singular estimation among and above all other nations; insomuch as let an Englishman be in company among people of sundry other nations, you shall have him admired of them all, yea, and both of man and woman more favored and respected, than any other in the company, as one that carrieth more courteous, friendly and lovely countenances before all other people.[6]

And a century after Camden the antiquary Aylett Sammes in 1676 showed a fierce geographical chauvinism when angrily rejecting attempts to argue a comparatively late insulation of Britain from the European land-mass, 'to make this Ancient and Renowned ISLAND, once a hanger-on, or part of the Continent'

> It was ever the Glory and Safety of *GREAT BRITAIN* to be environed by the Sea, and to command those Waters that encompass it . . . Nature has set *BRITAIN* such distinct Bounds and Limits, that its Empire is preserved entire and as it abounds in all things, both for the necessary delight and support of Man, and needs not the World to sustain it, so it was always esteemed . . . *a distinct WORLD by it self.*[7]

By the middle of the seventeenth century, the new spirit of intellectual enquiry on empirical foundations, as contrasted to the

ancient Aristotelian tradition, which was to bring the Royal Society
into being, was already acting as a ferment. John Aubrey was acutely
conscious of this break with the past and of his personal involvement
with the new studies of antiquity. He continued his 1685 comment on
what he saw as an 'innovation in learning'

> I was from my childhood affected with the view of things rare; which is the beginning
> of philosophy . . . I was carried on with a strong impulse to undertake this taske: I knew
> not why, unles for my owne private pleasure. Credit there was none; for it gets the
> disrespect of a man's neighbours. But I could not rest quiet till I had obeyed this secret
> call. Mr Camden, Dr Plott and Mr Wood confess the same.[8]

Anthony Wood, the Oxford antiquary, certainly shared an emotional
response to antiquities when he wrote in 1656, shifting from first to
third person as was his wont

> This summer came to Oxford '*The Antiquities of Warwickshire*' &c written by
> William Dugdale . . . my pen cannot enough describe how A.Wood's tender affections
> and insatiable desire of knowledge were ravish'd and melted downe by the reading of
> that book.[9]

Aubrey and Wood might quarrel, but both were sustained by vivid
inner convicions.

But by the early eighteenth century, as we have seen, antiquarian
studies suffered, in common with other historical disciplines, from a
decline which was to endure almost until its end, and it was perhaps
with a sense of desperation that Alexander Gordon, in the preface to
his *Itinerarium Septentrionale* of 1726, a description of Roman
antiquities in North Britain, mounted a spirited defence and castigated
the critics. 'Seeing Reason and Knowledge are Characteristics which
distinguish Mankind from the most ignoble Part of the Animal
Creation, those Studies, which are the most improving, deserve our
greatest application: In the Number of which, *Antiquity* claims a great
share, particularly *Archaiology*, which consists of Monuments, or
rather Inscriptions, still subsisting.' So far a temperate claim enough,
and Gordon continues a defence along the usual lines, but then his
anger breaks out and he rounds on his opponents

> I know, that there are people to be found, and it is to be regretted, some of them of Birth
> and Fortune, who expose their own Ignorance, in discountenancing this Kind of
> Knowledge, giving out, that Antiquity, and such like branches of Learning, are but the
> Chymeras of *Virtuosi*, dry and unpleasant searches; So, because they themselves are
> blind, and incapable to relish such Pleasures, they have the Imprudence to betray their
> own Weakness to the World. Hence, we observe, that things which are in their Nature

rough, unpolish'd, vicious and cruel, these fit their Genius the best, violent Hunting, Bear Gardens, Gaming-tables, Quarrelling, and Midnight Revellings, are their Darling Delights.

The antiquaries may have been going down by 1726, but some were going down fighting.

Antiquaries and archaeology

It is time to pause, and take stock, and to consider the main theme of this book, the application of archaeological means to the discovery of the pre-Roman past of Britain from the late sixteenth to the early nineteenth century. The antiquaries as revealed by the public's reaction to their foibles, certainly emerge as a very odd lot; dispassionate consideration of their achievement (which was considerable) show them as by no means a homogeneous body, but more mixed in methods and aims to our eyes today than to their contemporaries. By no means all the early antiquaries were contributing to the emergence and development of what we with hindsight recogize as archaeology; those who did are very much in the minority. In 1934 H.B. Walters published *The English Antiquaries of the sixteenth, seventeenth and eighteenth centuries*, a charming privately printed period piece, consisting of short biographical essays and still quoted in popular histories of archaeology. But of the couple of dozen characters rightly assembled as antiquaries, hardly more than four can be regarded as pursuing studies ancestral to archaeology, three only as prehistorians. In this distinction there is a reflection of what happened to these subjects in their early evolution, an internal division which is of particular importance for our present enquiry.

The first thing which strikes us today is that most who were regarded by their contemporaries, and themselves, as antiquaries in the seventeenth and eighteenth centuries, were in fact in varying degrees historians, using exclusively documentary sources for a study of the medieval or later past. Sir William Dugdale's *Antiquities of Warwickshire* of 1656, for instance, is a county history of what was to become a well-known type, with its evidence solely based on written records, and his famous *Monasticon* contained nothing of the architectural history of the religious houses, as the very concept of such a study was as yet unformed. Anthony Wood had proudly inscribed on his tombstone in 1695 ANTONIUS WOOD ANTIQUARIUS, but though he might sketch the ruins of Eynsham Abbey Church or Bampton Castle, and transcribe monumental inscriptions, 'his beloved studies of English History, Antiquities, Heraldry and Genealogies' were what he enumerated: documentary and mainly biographical. Thomas Hearne, lampooned as *the* antiquary in Pope's *Dunciad*, certainly made several visits to the newly discovered Roman pavement at Stonesfield in 1712, but his reputation rests on his editions of medieval chronicles.[10] The list could be easily extended, but the separation of what was considered the realm of the antiquaries from that of the historians goes back to the time of Leland and Camden. It was no accident that the Elizabethan society called itself that of antiquaries, though all its surviving papers show it to be exclusively concerned with historical studies of one sort or another, and with a strongly legal bias from a membership largely drawn from the Inns of Court. It was the nature of history, inherited by the Renaissance from classical antiquity, that separated it from the antiquarian approach: so well put by Trevor-Roper

To the humanists history was a rhetorical exercise. They used historical characters as ideal types, whether of moral virtue (or vice) or political *virtú*. They made politics depend on personalities, ascribed edifying or unedifying motives, and invented appropriate speeches. They set great store on an elegant Latin style. Indeed, they were more interested in style than in objective truth, for history to them had an ulterior purpose: it was 'philosophy teaching by examples' and the examples were chosen, or adjusted, to fit the philosophy.[11]

By Camden's time new traditions, those of 'civil history', were being created in France, notably by the great jurist Jean Bodin, whose *Modus ad facilem historiarum cognitionem* of 1566 was highly influential, and Camden demonstrated his masterly capacity not only as a new-style topographer-antiquary, but as one of the new History Men in his *Annals of Queen Elizabeth* (1615 and 1623). The new history needed new approaches to the records and the publication of accurate original texts; the new society coming into being in early modern England demanded a reassessment of the origins and privileges of institutions, both civil and ecclesiastical, and here antiquary and historian merged into one. At the more personal and family level, and with the social re-alignments of the period, a need arose for established families to re-affirm their dominant place in the hierarchy, for others to establish themselves for the first time, and as a result genealogy and its demonstration in heraldry became irresistibly popular. The College of Arms, its origins going back to the late fifteenth century, took on an enhanced importance as the official guardian and authenticator of pedigrees and armorial bearings, held in high esteem as a visual statement of rank and status; 'the sixteenth and seventeenth centuries probably saw the most widespread and general understanding of heraldry which has ever been known in this realm'.[12] Here the antiquaries came into their own, and heraldry and antiquarianism became virtually synonymous: Camden held office as Clarenceux king of arms from 1597 to his death in 1623; Dugdale was proclaimed Garter king of arms in 1667, to name two only of the College among the antiquaries.

It is obvious that antiquarian pursuits should be regarded as trifling by the historians of the old school, devoted to the grand manner and the presentation of the great and good of the past as moral exemplars. And this tradition died hard, forming as it did a key position held by the Ancients in their battle against the Moderns, as one of the main protagonists for antiquity, Sir William Temple, made clear in 1695, arguing that history should not concern itself with matters that 'neither argue the Virtues or Vices of Princes nor Serve for Example or Instruction to Posterity, which are the great ends of History and ought to be the chief Care of all historians'.[13] Here there was clearly no place for the antiquaries with their charters and obscure chroniclers, none for the College of Arms. And still less could Roman pavements and pottery, coins and inscriptions, be accounted as anything but irrelevant trivia, while the ancient Briton with his miserable stone tools and rude monuments could by no stretch of the imagination 'Serve for Example or Instruction to Posterity.'

In the traditional world of polite learning there was no place for the study of the past by means of its material culture which was fundamental to the emergence of the discipline of what has been distinguished as either text-aided or text-free archaeology: in the present instance the study of Roman Britain or of its prehistoric antecedents. To do this required a novel conceptual approach to potential evidence for the past. As R.G. Collingwood put it, 'prehistoric flints or Roman pottery acquire the posthumous character of historical evidence, not because the men who made them thought of them as historical evidence, but because *we* think of them as historical evidence.'[14] It demanded not an appeal to authority, a search for support in the opinions of revered figures of the past, nor in the application of *a priori* reasoning such as that of antiquity, but a fresh unprejudiced examination of things themselves with the aim of seeking explanation from them by processes of inductive reason. Such a new conceptual awareness was to be implicit in that great event of the English seventeenth century, the Intellectual Revolution; in its simplest form the ideas inspired by Francis Bacon and put into practice by those who formed the Royal Society in the second half of the century.

Of course in fact this novel intellectual adventure, which was to re-model all thinking and give us, for good or ill, the modern world we mentally inhabit today, was by no means simple. Its origins and growth, its early affiliations in political and religious terms, its content and achievements, its pretentions and its fallacies, its status in the history of science and of philosophy, have been the subject of an intimidatingly large literature.[15] Our own purpose, to seek in the new philosophy evidence for its favouring or discouraging the beginnings of what was to become recognizable as archaeology, has itself been the subject of important specialist studies, notably those of Michael Hunter, and here we can do no more than gratefully acknowledge the help these give us in reviewing the questions once again. But to anticipate, the genesis of archaeology and prehistory is to be found uniquely in the new science, the Baconians, the Men of Gresham, the Virtuosi of the Royal Society; laughed at or ignored by the contemporary literary gentlemen, the Wits, who made little attempt to master or even understand the intellectual position of their ultimately successful opponents.

One of the simpler but fundamental procedures of the new science was the empirical approach to phenomena, natural or man-made, in terms of objective observation, description and interpretation, especially in the form of classification and ordering. On the one hand there were the obvious fields of Natural Histories of stones, plants or animals; on the other Artificial Histories of contemporary technology, the Histories of Trades to which much attention was paid in the seventeenth century from Samuel Hartlib and his circle, to others later: in both, it must be remembered, 'History' meaning an enquiry of the phenomena, with no necessary chronological overtones. The construction of such Histories, it was widely held by the new philosophers, could be the task of a comparatively short duration, and their completion would display the phenomenal universe, the works of God and of Man, in a comprehensible and amenable form, ready for further definition by the great new intellectual tool of the age, mathematics.

These are all factors especially associated with the formal founding of the Royal Society in 1660. But the climate of opinion in which such thinking became possible was already established and found congenial by before the mid-century – it is worth remembering that the familiar phrase 'climates of opinion' was invented by Joseph Glanvill, one of the first Fellows and a zealous apologist of the Society.

It represents a new idea, breaking away from the unconscious concept of a unitary world view in favour of intellectual diversity which could flourish or wither according to circumstances, and very much embodied the spirit of the times. And it was exactly in such a climate of opinion that a part of the now established antiquarianism could break away and grope towards a new discipline that was eventually, but not before the late nineteenth century, to become archaeology rather than antiquarianism.

The concern of antiquarianism from the beginning, as the jokes show, was with objects as well as written texts, and one difficult of comprehension to a scholarly culture based solely on literary sources for its knowledge of antiquity; a culture enlivened by the contemplation, by a gentleman of correct taste, of works of sculpture or monumental architecture in approved modes. The gallery of works of art was not to be compared with the cabinet of curiosities such as that of an antiquary like Sir Thomas Browne, 'his whole house and garden being a paradise and cabinet of rarities . . . especially medails, books, plants and natural things' as John Evelyn recorded in 1671, or Tradescant's Ark with its Naturals and Artificials, which came to Oxford in 1683 as Elias Ashmole's gift, as part of the equipment of an alchemical laboratory, the Ashmolean Museum. The Royal Society's own museum, catalogued in 1681 by the botanist Nehemiah Grew, included not only natural history specimens but 'Coins and other matters relating to Antiquity', and among the fossils and crystals as 'Regular Stones', prehistoric flint arrowheads (as in contemporary and earlier Renaissance collections on the Continent). Here, cherished in collections which were those not of art, but artifacts; those put on an equal footing with plants, animals and fossils as the subject-matter of classification and taxonomy, was the tangible evidence of antiquarian investigation, Collingwood's objects thought of as evidence.[16] From antiquities in the museum to monuments in the field was an obvious step in the world of the new topographers, and the kinship between some at least of the early antiquaries who were breaking away from documents and heraldry, was appreciated by those who were beginning to justify the title of scientist in the Royal Society. Thomas Sprat, Bishop of Rochester and combative supporter of the new science, wrote in his 1667 *History of the Royal Society* that under its aegis

Many things that have been hitherto hidden will arise and expose themselves to view . . . nay, even many *Rarities* of *Antiquity* will be hereby restor'd. Of these a great quantity have been overwhelm'd in the ruins of *Time*; and they will sooner be retriev'd by our labouring anew in the material subjects whence they first arose, than by our plodding everlastingly on the ancient *Writings*.[17]

The great Robert Hooke in 1668 made the point of convergence between the study of palaeontology and archaeology explicit when he 'elaborated an analogy between fossil shells, as marks of the former extent of the sea, and Roman coins as marks of the extent of an ancient empire', and went on to place in parallel the tasks of the 'Natural Antiquary' studying geology and fossils and the student of 'Artificial' antiquities such as coins and medals.[18] The metaphor was not forgotten by geologists: Gideon Mantell's best-seller of 1844 was entitled *The Medals of Creation, or First Lessons in Geology*.

The first archaeologically minded antiquaries then were those who deliberately rejected much of their traditional subject-matter to concentrate on the actual objects of antiquity, and particularly, since from the days of Camden topography formed an integral part of antiquarian studies, to monuments in the countryside. What with hindsight we conceive of as the beginnings of real archaeology in Britain was inseparably bound up with fieldwork, not with studies in museums. Robert Plot (1640–96), whom we shall encounter again, did not even think of himself as an antiquarian, but as an investigator of the natural history of the English counties, perhaps on the lines proposed by Robert Boyle to the Royal Society in 1666 under the 'General Heads for the Natural History of a Countrey'. Plot produced such Natural Histories for two counties, Oxfordshire in 1677, Staffordshire in 1686, and in each there is a separate chapter *Of Antiquities*, which, he has to explain, is perhaps not what might be expected, and he has to set out

for the Satisfaction of the *Reader*, upon what terms I add this *Chapter* of *Antiquities* to my *Natural History*, it seeming to some altogether forraigne to the purpose. I take leave to acquaint him, before I advance any further, that I intend not to meddle with the *pedigrees* or *descents* either of *families* or *lands* . . . . nor the *antiquities* or *foundations* of *Religious houses*.[19]

This sounds like a reference to Dugdale, and Plot goes on (in both his volumes) to enumerate instead antiquities, 'Such as ancient *Money*, *Ways*, *Barrows*, *Pavements*, *Urns*, ancient *Monuments* of Stone, *Fortifications*, &c'.[20]

We are in a new world, that of the monuments of Roman and pre-Roman Britain, and while the latter alone form the main concern of this book, it is worth looking at the explicit statements of two antiquaries devoted wholly to Roman Britain in the 1720s. Roman archaeology, of course, had highly respectable roots in the Italian Renaissance as we saw, and even the remains of the remote British province of the Empire long continued to share something of the esteem attributed to classical studies of literature and art, a mystique enduring to this day. It had a foot in both camps, the prestige of the Ancients combined with the techniques of the Moderns. Alexander Gordon, whose spirited defence of archaeology in his *Itinerarium Septrionale* of 1726 has already been quoted, made it clear in his Preface that his object was 'to prove and illustrate these Passages and Actions of their own Roman Historians, by the Monuments of Antiquity which I have found concerning them', 'I confess' he writes, 'I have not spar'd any Pain in tracing the Footsteps of the *Romans*, and in drawing and measuring all the Figures in the following Sheets from the Originals, having made a pretty laborious Progress through almost every part of *Scotland* for three years successively.' John Horsley (1684–1732) was a great scholar, immeasurably superior to Gordon, whose *Britannia Romana* of 1732 was largely written in 1727–29 partly to correct the errors in Gordon's book, and emerged as a majestic contribution to learning. He too is at pains to stress in his Preface the new fieldwork behind the great corpus in his second part: the first part, he says, 'cost me much labour and time in my study', but Book II 'was the most expensive and tedious. Several thousand miles were travelled on this account, to visit ancient monuments, and re-examine them, where there was any doubt or difficulty . . . Some perhaps may be inclined to censure me, for having spent so much time on subjects, which by many will be thought of no importance . . .' ''Tis certainly more commendable' he goes on with a touch of Gordon's spleen 'for gentlemen of estates, and persons of quality, to spend their time in the prosecution of such entertaining knowledge, than either in idleness, or vicious pleasures.'

The students of ancient Britain

Two students of Roman Britain, Gordon and Horsley, are worth quoting for their complete emancipation from the traditional stereo- type of the antiquary in favour of a single-minded attention to a limited archaeological objective and for their explicit and vigorous defence of field studies for this purpose. Our direct concern is with those who in the earlier generations following Camden and in the intellectually favourable atmosphere leading up to and culminating in the establishment of the Royal Society, similarly broke away from the old uncritical and omnivorous antiquarianism, not to text-aided archaeology in the study of Roman Britain, but the text-free archaeology of pre-Roman times and of the ancient Britons. Robert Plot (1640–96) wrote his chapters on Antiquities in deliberate rejection of documentary sources, and included British coins and stone and bronze implements: Gordon in fact also illustrated prehistoric bronzes and both thought them Roman. The great figures devoting themselves to prehistoric antiquity and studying monuments in the field at first hand were three – John Aubrey (1626–97), Edward Lhuyd (1660–1709) and William Stukeley (1687–1765). Minor figures include Henry Rowlands (1655–1723) and (on the grounds of a few days' field work) Francis Wise (1695–1767). Later in the eighteenth century we have only William Borlase (1695–1772), since Stukeley's field work was over, and his sounder judgment largely suspended, by 1726. In Scotland credit must go to Sir Robert Sibbald (1641–1722) for publishing with illustrations Bronze Age metalwork and pots, even if inevitably he regarded them as Roman.

It is not the purpose of the present book to treat the early study of prehistoric Britain in terms of the biographies of the individual antiquaries, but rather to consider their contributions to the composite picture pieced together over nearly two centuries from their work, and from others not working in the field, and from beliefs and assumptions about the past of quite different, literary, origins. Extended biographies of the major figures have in fact been published; of Aubrey by Anthony Powell and Michael Hunter, of William Stukeley by the present writer and of Borlase by Peter Pool, though sadly Edward Lhuyd still lacks adequate published consideration.[21] Here for our present purpose it will be sufficient to sketch the work of those main figures, especially those of the first heroic generation whose contributions were made before the fateful intellectual slump around 1730, when Borlase (not in himself of any real outstanding distinction) held the flickering torch of prehistoric studies for the rest of the eighteenth century.

John Aubrey's reputation, like his life, has been chequered, inconsistent and at times unfortunate. His biographical sketches, the *Brief Lives*, were never forgotten by the literary world, but regarded as 'quaint', and by the nineteenth century some, alas, indelicate, while the publication of his *Miscellanies* in 1696 and the *Remains of Gentilisme and Judaisme* in 1881 encouraged a view of him as a credulous, whimsical old man to whom Anthony Wood's bitchy phrase 'magotieheaded' was all too frequently applied. Archaeologists had however thought better of Aubrey, and since John Britton published his *Memoir* of him in 1845, Jackson his *Wiltshire Collections* in 1862, and Long his Avebury notes and plans from the *Monumenta Britannica* MS in 1858–62, had recognized his outstanding merits as a pioneer fieldworker, and the unique value of the *Monumenta*. In 1948 Powell established Aubrey as a Restoration scholar and man of letters to be taken seriously and sympathetically, and Hunter's 1975 study convincingly placed him as an outstanding figure in the world of contemporary science, including archaeology. Aubrey's main contribution to prehistory was in the form of the *Temple Druidum* section, a first-hand description of Avebury, Stonehenge and other stone circles, and further chapters on earthworks and barrows. Edmund Gibson printed a summary in his great 1695 edition of Camden's *Britannia* and so something of Aubrey's work became known to the learned world; Stukeley as we shall see based his own fieldwork in Wiltshire entirely on that of Aubrey.

Stonehenge had become the subject of a sterile little controversy in mid-century between the great architect Inigo Jones in his *Stone-Heng* (1655), claiming it as a Roman temple, Walter Charleton, a fashionable court physician, counter-claiming it as a Danish coronation place in his *Chorea Gigantum* of 1663, and John Webb an architect and relative of Jones's who had edited the *Stone-Heng* replying for the Romans in a *Vindication* (1665). All relied on literary sources except Jones, whose plans of the monument were shamelessly altered from reality to fit his theories.

Robert Plot would have regarded himself as a natural philosopher, though his contributions to archaeology were not inconsiderable. In Oxford, soon after 1660, he put up to the famous Dr John Fell, then Dean of Christ Church, an absurdly grandiose scheme, which could only have been conceived by the bumptious rather rich young man in his early 20s that Plot was, proposing 'a personal ten years' topographical survey of England and Wales 'for the Discovery of Antiquities and other Curiosities'. This (with very much else) would include 'a full Collection of *British, Roman, Saxon* and ancient *English* Money . . . likewise of Urns, Lamps, Lachrymatories . . . also of *British, Roman* or *Saxon* Fortifications . . . *Barberry-Castle in Wilts* . . . *Silbery Hill* . . . the Barrows of the Downes in *Wilts*, at *Ollantigh* in *Kent* and other Places.' In a modified form he did in fact produce his Natural Histories of Oxfordshire and Staffordshire in 1667 and 1686 with their separate chapters on antiquities. He was Secretary of the Royal Society in 1682, and in the following year first Keeper of the Ashmolean Museum in Oxford (by virtue it seems more of his alchemy than his archaeology), a post he retained until 1690, when he was succeeded by Edward Lhuyd, his Under-Keeper. Plot had become Historiographer Royal in 1688, a sinecure first held by James Howell in 1661; Dryden held it in 1670 and Plot was followed by the first real historian in the office, Thomas Rymer. Plot deserves re-assessment. He acquired a reputation for credulity and was certainly much given to prodigies and monsters: one regrets not having the account of 'Strange People, such as the *Gubbings* in *Devonshire*, the People of *Charleton-Curley* in *Leycester-shire*' he promised Dr Fell, but he did some sound original fieldwork on the ring-ditches in the meadows of North Oxford.[22]

His successor in the Ashmolean, Edward Lhuyd, was a polymath of quite exceptional brilliance, who hated Plot with a vehemence surprising in such a generous and gentle scholar.[23] He wrote in 1691 to Martin Lister on Plot's retirement of 'this happy delivery out of his clutches; for (to give him his due) I think he's a man of as bad morals as ever took a doctor's degree. I wish his wife a good bargain of him, & to myself yt I may never meet with ye like again' – Plot had just married a wealthy widow. Lhuyd first distinguished himself as a pioneer palaeontologist, and though he did not consider them as extinct organisms, he published in 1699 the *Lithophylacii Britannia Ichonographia*, a systematic catalogue illustrating nearly 2,000 fossils, at a time when he had already made outstanding contributions as a botanist to the mountain flora of the British Isles. Simultaneously, from 1693 he had been enrolled by Edmund Gibson to revise the Welsh entries for the new edition of Camden's *Britannia* which appeared triumphantly in 1695, and had embarked on his own independent *Archaeologia Britannica, giving some account . . . of the Languages Histories and Customs of the Original Inhabitants of Great Britain*, of which only the first volume, the *Glossography*, was published in 1707, two years before his unexpected death. The first volume, setting out the vocabularies and grammars of Irish, Welsh, Cornish and Breton, with a penetrating analysis of their relationships, was a work of comparative philology of such staggering brilliance that at one stroke it set such studies on a foundation only to be built on by modern scholarship from the 1850s, and one can but guess at the quality of the unwritten 'Account of all such Monuments now remaining in *Wales*, as are presumed to be *British*' which was to follow. The 1695 *Britannia* gives us a glimpse of its potential; for the rest, the posthumous history of Lhuyd's papers, subject to every disastrous vicissitude of dispersal, destruction and disappearance, has deprived us of what could have been the outstanding contribution to archaeology of the later seventeenth century.

A word must here be said of Aylett Sammes, who in 1676 published his *Britannia Antiqua Illustrata*, dealing with the colonization of prehistoric Britain by Phoenicians (and some Cimbri and Greeks). Little is known of the author, a lawyer who took absolutely no notice of the evidence of material culture, but his vigorous, lengthy, incoherent and wholly misleading book attracted much contemporary attention and was to have a surprising influence on subsequent ideas about prehistory.[24]

This is a convenient place to review these early contributions to archaeology, rather than to an uncritical antiquarianism, and their relation to the early decades of the Royal Society. Boyle's scheme of 1666 for Natural Histories led to an important aspect of research in the documentation of natural and artificial topographical phenomena, including antiquities: the circulation of questionnaires by the compilers to informed recipients.[25] This, an early example of what has become known in natural history as 'network research', was extensively developed in the 1670s and 80s: John Ogilby 'His Majesty's Cosmographer' in 1673, Thomas Machell of Queen's College Oxford in 1676; Richard Parsons Chancellor of Gloucester about the same time, Robert Plot 1674 and 1678, John Aubrey 1675–80 and Edward Lhuyd in 1707 all circulated Parochial Enquiries to the clergy and gentry of the areas with which they were concerned in order to broaden the basis of their own observations. This was corpus-making in the Royal Society tradition of Lhuyd's catalogue of fossils, Martin Lister's *Historia Animalium* (1678) and *Historia methodica . . . conchylorum* (1691: on molluscan shells), or John Ray's *Historia Plantarum* (1686–1704). It was within this favourable atmosphere, if not strictly within the ambit of the Society itself, that an objective archaeology based on first-hand record of artifacts in the field or collections was just emerging, and in the context of the New Science. Hunter has shown how from about 1680 the *Philosophical Transactions* of the Royal Society began to publish articles on antiquities, mainly Roman but often of high objective value, and continued to do so until the first decade of the eighteenth century.[26]

But by now the Royal Society was changing its character. From the time of the publication in 1687 of Newton's *Principia*, it has been observed, 'a hiatus became apparent between the lofty Newtonian sciences and the humble non-mathematical sciences, and these began to lose social prestige'. Newton was elected President of the Society in 1703 and contrived to remain so for twenty-five years. His prestige was unassailable, his mathematics revered by all if understood by few, but the other activities of the Society now became contemptuously dismissed or openly derided. Already by 1694 William Wooton had deplored that 'the Humour of the Age, as to these things, is visibly altered from what it was Twenty or Thirty years ago' and scientific studies the victims of 'the sly insinuations of the *Men of Wit*' and wrote of 'the *public ridiculing* of all those who spend their Time and Fortunes in seeking after what some call useless Natural Rarities'.[27] John Locke in 1690 loftily conceded that 'it is necessary in the learned age' for a gentleman to study natural philosophy 'to fit himself for conversation', but Addison in 1710 felt it to be 'the Mark of a little Genius to be wholly conversant among Insects . . . and those trifling Rarities that furnish the Apartment of a Virtuoso'.[28] The war was declared, the Wits against the Virtuosi, Ancients against Moderns; literary gentlemen against unlettered scientists. We are not surprised that Thomas Shadwell put on a satirical play *The Virtuoso* in 1676, ridiculing the natural philosophers of the Royal Society in the figure of Sir Nicolas Gimcrack, though not specifically the antiquaries. It was reprinted in 1704 and is in the tradition of Shackerley Marmion and John Gay's farce of 1717.

There was reaction within the Royal Society itself, and as early as 1689 a group of up to forty Fellows formed the unofficial Temple Coffee House Botanic Club, including in its membership notable figures in botany and natural history such as Hans Sloane, Martin Lister, Nehemiah Grew and many others, and continuing to flourish at least until 1712.[29] By this time a movement wholly unconnected with the Royal Society was bringing together representatives of quite different interests, the antiquaries, who consciously looking back to their Elizabethan Society, re-founded themselves in 1717 as the Society of Antiquaries of London.[30] Unlike the Botanic Club, this in no way represented the new world of learning, but rather a return to the cosy, out-of-date pursuits of Earle's satire, with Norroy king of arms as President, and Richmond Herald as a founder member, and though the list included the great palaeographical scholar Humphrey Wanley, among the nonentities was Browne Willis, 'Old Wrinkle-boots'[31], in his own lifetime a caricature of the old-fashioned eccentric antiquary. One figure alone stands out as a belated example of the Baconian, Royal Society approach to antiquity, and almost its greatest exponent: William Stukeley, the Antiquaries' first Secretary.

His life and work are exceptionally well documented and one sees clearly the division of his career into two phases, the first as a physician and the second as an Anglican clergyman. Born in 1687, ten years before Aubrey's death, he obtained in 1717–18, at a time when he was already interesting himself in antiquities (and as we have seen, taking part in the foundation of the new Society), a transcript of the major part of the *Monumenta Britannica* MS made by the great scholar, Thomas Gale, Dean of York, about 1697. Although Stukeley (rather disingenuously) never admitted his debt to Aubrey's MS, its first-hand descriptions and plans of the great stone monuments of Avebury and Stonehenge in Wiltshire formed the inspiration and basis for his own remarkable programme of fieldwork and record at the two sites on which his reputation rested in his lifetime and on which it is even more securely based today. Following Aubrey he brought the by now almost extinct tradition of empirical fieldwork of the Royal Society group of Aubrey himself, Plot and Lhuyd, to bear on the great stone circles and allied monuments by intensive survey between 1718 and 1725 at the two major monuments, and by extensive tours in the English countryside; in 1723 he wrote up the Stonehenge and Avebury work for publication,[32] but though he published his tours as *Itinerarium Curiosum* in the following year, *Stonehenge* did not appear in print until 1740, *Abury* in 1743. By then Dr Stukeley was the Reverend Dr Stukeley, having taken clerical orders in 1729, and given up fieldwork. He indulged in very un-Baconian speculations on the Druids for which in fact he was to be best known until the 1920s; his real contribution to British archaeology was unrecognized until O.G.S. Crawford discovered the potential of the manuscript sources still fortunately surviving.

Stukeley had helped to found the Society of Antiquaries in 1717, and was its energetic Secretary until in 1726 he left London for the country and, before long, ordination. It seems clear that he was disappointed in the lack of response he found in the new Society for Roman and pre-Roman studies, and in 1722 formed a club, The Society of Roman Knights, to further these aims. But it was too late. The climate of opinion was against him. The 1720s were not the 1680s. History itself, and the natural sciences including, for instance, geomorphology and palaeontology, with which archaeology was beginning to develop an alliance in the Royal Society, all fell into decline around 1730. The naturalists showed more resilience than the antiquaries during the eighteenth century, for archaeology did not really recover for a century and a half.

One last figure, even more isolated in a changed intellectual world than Stukeley, must be considered, William Borlase (1695–1772). He was a naturalist–antiquary, a Cornish parson holding livings near Penzance, elected to the Royal Society as a naturalist and publishing his *Natural History of Cornwall* in 1758, but four years earlier the *Antiquities of Cornwall*. Despite some odd Druidical aberrations, this was a conscientious piece of original observation and record without parallel at its date and representing the last of the Restoration tradition of good archaeological fieldwork: it looked back rather than forward. Borlase's isolation was not his physical residence in Cornwall – he exploited his intimate knowledge of the Duchy to the full – but intellectual. He did his best by keeping up his Oxford contacts (he had gone up to Exeter College in 1713) but the only antiquaries he could correspond with were Francis Wise, Radcliffe Librarian and a dabbler in antiquities, and young William Huddesford, Keeper of the Ashmolean at twenty-three through the blatant nepotism of his father; not an impressive pair, but there were no rivals. In London there were Charles Lyttleton and Jeremiah Milles, successively Deans of Exeter and Fellows of the Society of Antiquaries, of which Milles became President in 1768; here again neither was a scholar of any standing, but all too representative of what passed as the world of antiquarian learning: Samuel Foote's farce ridiculing the Society in session came out during Milles's presidency in 1771. Stukeley was by now deep in Druidic fantasies. Poor Borlase in his isolation shows all too well the barrenness of the land around him.

It is, then, with these antiquaries from Camden onwards, and with other minor figures who turned to the subject of pre-Roman Britain and its peoples, that this book is concerned, and in subsequent chapters their individual contributions to the subject, largely from the monuments and artifacts themselves, will be brought together. But we must avoid importing into the past of the sixteenth to eighteenth centuries our own ideas about archaeology, prehistory and history. The world picture of educated men in these centuries was emphatically not ours, and the world picture was one which included the past as well as the present. Here the conditioning factors were, as they had been from antiquity, the authority of the written texts of what were so often referred to, with admiration and respect, as The Ancient Authors. Of these written authorities one had dominated Western Christianity from its inception, the texts of the Old and New Testaments of the Bible, and these assumed a new urgency and validity with the Reformation and their translation into the vernacular. For the early antiquity of man one Ancient Author stood as supreme authority in men's minds, Moses, the author of the Book of Genesis and the rest of the Pentateuch. To Moses (and other less reputable sources) we must now turn in order to understand the past as the early antiquaries were unconsciously conditioned by their education and background to think about it.

The seventeenth century would have approved. ''Tis the Sacred Writings of Scripture that are the best monuments of Antiquity' wrote Thomas Burnet in his Theory of the Earth of 1684,[33] and in the next year John Edwards, in *A Discourse concerning the Authority Stile and Perfection of the Old and New Testaments* even more explicitly directs our way

Scriptures are the greatest Monuments of Antiquity that are extant in the whole World . . . A prying Antiquary may find more Work and much to his Advantage in the Writings of the Old Testament, especially in the Five Books of Moses, than in all the Mouldy Manuscripts and Records in the whole world besides.[34]

2

The ancient authors: Eden to Ararat

A controlling factor in the thought of all who were concerned with the early past of man, from classical antiquity to the nineteenth century, was the authority of written sources; a factor all the more potent to those who wrote and those who read about early man for being on the whole accepted without question as an inevitable axiom. When Samuel Johnson made his often quoted pronouncement – 'All that is really known of the ancient state of Britain is contained in a few pages. We can know no more than what old writers have told us'[1] – he was not speaking as a reactionary die-hard but as a fair representative of educated thought which would have been acceptable up to and indeed after his time. No alternatives had been put forward, for however much Aubrey, Lhuyd or Stukeley may have looked at field monuments and stone and bronze tools, they had not formulated the concept of Collingwood's unconscious evidence only interpreted as such by the modern observer, and so had never presented such a view to others.

The requirements of an authority on the past were an accepted text by a named individual, the latter providing a comprehensible personality to validate the former. The past was the past of persons, history a recital of their acts written by others, as part of the construction of a tradition peculiar to a particular social unit which consolidated and reinforced its identity in the present by providing a chronological dimension of continuity and so of reassurance. The Greeks, and following them the Romans, were concerned with their recent history; the former happily accepted mythical figures such as Heracles or Atreus as founders of historically extant lines of descent, and both left the remoter past of man to the imagination of the poets, Hesiod or Lucretius, in the realm of philosophical speculation, and inconceivable of resolution by any other means.

The authority of Moses

From the third century BC the Hellenistic world was made aware of a new and alien type of history with the translation into Greek of the Semitic texts forming the sacred books of the Jews, probably made in Alexandria and traditionally the work of 70 (or 72) scholars, from which it took its name of the Septuagint (LXX). These Hebrew and Greek versions in turn became the Old Testament of the Christian faith, and it is in this form that it was to dominate Western thought on the earliest history of mankind for nearly two millennia. It presented history not only as the supernatural manifestation of an unique single God, but as a unilinear sequential and episodic narrative, documenting and validating the choice by Yahweh of a restricted tribe of people, the Jews, as the recipients of exclusive divine favour (and disfavour). In this chronicle there could be no prehistoric time, because it opened with the creation of the world by divine fiat, a creation culminating in man himself, thus replacing the classical speculations on infinite or cyclical time by an historical time-sequence with a fixed beginning. For Jews and Christians alike this new scheme was a sacred text beyond criticism, let alone contradiction, and more secular authority was lent to its earliest section by a named author. The first five books of the Old Testament – Genesis, Exodus, Leviticus, Numbers, Deuteronomy, collectively the Pentateuch – were believed to have been written under divine inspiration by the Jew Moses, whose death brings the Pentateuch to a close. So far as the non-Jewish, Gentile, world was concerned, and for students of early man in Europe and the British Isles, the essential historical facts, taken as such without any necessary theological implications, were contained in the book of Genesis, from the Creation, through Eden to the Fall and Expulsion, the increasing sinfulness culminating in the retribution of a provoked Yahweh in the form of the Flood, and the subsequent peopling of a devastated post-diluvial world by the descendants of Noah.

In the early Christian world Latin translations of the Old and New Testaments appeared, and about AD 382, at the instance of the Pope Damasus, the great scholar St Jerome undertook a definitive Latin translation using for the Old Testament not only the Greek LXX but essentially the original Hebrew text. This Latin version of the Bible, the *versio vulgata* or Vulgate, was accepted as canonical by the medieval church in the West. In the Reformed churches, translations into local vernaculars were produced, culminating in the English Protestant Churches, with the Authorized Version sponsored by King James I in

1611 and carried out by a band of ecclesiastical scholars who, in their supreme masterpiece of contemporary English prose, achieved the only major work of art to be the product of a committee.

From this time the Authorized Version was to dominate the thinking of all literate members of the Protestant faith in Britain. By reason of its supernatural authority and the compelling majesty of its prose it became a part of everyone's mental life, but quite apart from this, as a sheer historical document antedating all others it took an undisputed place among the writings of all other ancient authors. As we shall see, from the early formative patristic phase of Christianity serious scholarly effort was directed to constructing an absolute chronology in secular years from the Creation onwards which would embrace all other computations of the ancient world and form a definitive system of reference of universal application. The acceptance in some form or other of the Genesis narrative, from Adam to Noah, as a valid document of ancient history, was not, as has often been thought, a piece of religious obscurantism imposed upon and stultifying a scientific view of the antiquity of man, but rather an understandable reluctance to jettison what appeared to be a potentially valuable and informative historical text. The position was put with sobriety and authority in the nineteenth century by William Whewell, the Cambridge mathematician and scientist (he deserves the title, as he himself invented the word). Writing in 1837, the year in which he became President of the Geological Society, and in the context of the 'Mosaical account of the deluge,' he went on 'it would be as absurd to disregard the most ancient historical record, in attempting to trace back the history of the earth, as it would be gratuitously to reject any other source of information.'[2] The overthrow of this authority, later in the century, was due not so much to the puzzled and pious geologists as to the development of scholarly criticism of the Biblical text by German and later English theologians.

The construction of an absolute chronology goes back to Eusebius (*c.* AD 260–340), the Greek Bishop of Caesarea. The original of his short chronicle does not survive, but St Jerome (*c.* AD 348–420) used it for his Latin chronicle in AD 380–81, which was to endure as the fundamental basis until modern times. Both in the Middle Ages, and increasingly after the Reformation, variant individual chronologies were worked out, and indeed in 1759 a contemporary writer estimated that there were between seventy and seventy-five such 'systems of the age of the world' current in his time.[3] All reckoned from the beginning of time, from the Creation, *Anno Mundi*: the convention of counting years from the birth of Christ (AD) was first used by Dionysus Exiguus, who died about AD 540, but its complementary convention, 'BC' is of more recent date: Stukeley for instance does not use this abbreviation, though he does use 'AD' and 'AM' (*Anno Mundi*). 'BC' was used only intermittently in the eighteenth century, usually in abbreviated chronological tables. The official Russian calendar dated *Anno Mundi* until AD 1700, and it is amusing to note that today the scientists using radiometric and similar methods for dating the earth's (and mankind's) antiquity have abandoned the BC/AD convention in favour of BP (Before Present: nominally AD 1950), while the archaeologists still favour the dual division.

The Eusebius/Jerome computation gave a Creation date of 5200 BC, or alternatively, on a 'short chronology', 3964 BC. In the Middle Ages other schemes were sometimes proposed, using for instance not the generation-count of the long-lived patriarchs in Genesis 5, but the genealogy of Christ back to Adam in Matthew 1:17 or (for the six days of the Creation) the statement in Psalm 90, 'a thousand years in thy sight are but yesterday'. In the Reformation the subject aroused intense interest, prompted in part in England by millennarian expectations of those who, thrilled and excited by the prophecies of the Book of Daniel and ecstatically bewildered by the eschatology of the Book of Revelation, fuelled their fantasies by constructing chronologies not only of God's working in the past, but in a providentially ordained future. After the Restoration this fervour died down, though as late as 1746 William Whiston, Newton's successor in the Lucasian Chair of Mathematics at Cambridge and a friend of Stukeley's, proclaimed that the millennium was only twenty years away.[4] But a lot of serious scholarship was devoted to the subject in the seventeenth century; J.J. Scaliger published his *De emendatione temporum* in 1593, his *Eusebii Thesaurus Temporum* in 1606, and in England (or rather Ireland) James Ussher, Archbishop of Armagh (1581–1656), a great and scholarly historian, spent a lifetime on what became the standard chronology of the Old Testament and the ancient world, in his *Annalium* (1650 and 1654), and *Annales veteris testamenti* which appeared posthumously in 1659. This was printed in the margin of the Authorized Version in an edition of 1701 by William Lloyd, Bishop of Worcester, and thence became of almost canonical authority itself, with its famous Creation date of 4004 BC, though simultaneously, in 1659, Isaac Vossius had come up with one of 5400 BC on the evidence of the Septuagint rather than the Hebrew text.[5] For the antiquaries, the date of creation and the duration of its six days, with all its enormous problems, was the concern less of the students of early man than of the cosmological theorists such as Thomas Burnet or John Woodward; for the antiquaries as historians the critical event was the Flood and the subsequent re-peopling of the newly emergent world, an event generally agreed from the seventeenth century onwards to have been between about 2500 and 2000 BC.

This Old Testament chronology was the result of painstaking research, using not only the most sophisticated historical techniques then available, but turning to science for confirmation. This again was not the work of theological die-hards: the problems arose in the minds of those who were inevitably believers in a traditional faith as well as eagerly accepting the new knowledge becoming available within the Baconian school of thought. Napier of Merchiston, the inventor of logarithms, welcomed them 'as a short cut to calculating the Number of the Beast' in Revelations; Ussher himself consulted the mathematician Henry Briggs of Gresham College on the calculations involved in dating the solar eclipses of Biblical times; Newton (much concerned with these problems) used the precession of the equinox in writing his *Chronology of Ancient Kingdoms Amended* (1728); Stukeley turned to Edmond Halley the Astronomer Royal for details of the variations in the magnetic compass when computing the dates of Stonehenge and Avebury in the 1740s.[6]

Moses as the author of the Pentateuch was an accepted fact in the early Christian tradition from his role as Divine Law-Giver (John 1:45, 'we have found him, of whom Moses in the law, and the prophets did write'; Romans 10:5, 'For Moses describeth the righteousness which is of the law'). As such, he appeared the most ancient writer known and therefore superior in this respect, quite apart from his unique supernatural authority, to all others. But from the days of the early Church Fathers there had been current a belief, to be strongly reinforced in humanistic thought from the fifteenth century, in a pagan philosopher of great authority who was either nearly contemporary with Moses (whose death at the age of 120 Ussher had put at 1451 BC) or even more ancient, whose mystical writings survived. This brings us to thrice-great Hermes, Hermes Trismegistus, who appeared to rival Moses in authority.[7]

Thrice-great Hermes

From Herodotus onwards, the classical world regarded the Egyptians as having the most ancient tradition and fund of wisdom of all antiquity. The Egyptian god of learning and letters, Thoth, was equated with the Greek god Hermes, and philosophers like Cicero could write that Hermes 'gave letters and laws to the Egyptians'. A large body of mystical writings attributed to Hermes came into circulation from patristic times onwards, the most celebrated being the Latin *Asclepius*, attributed to Apuleius, and known for instance to Lactantius in the third and St Augustine in the fourth century AD, the former admiring him as a Gentile seer who foresaw Christianity, and even the latter admitting to his knowledge of the true God and dating him three generations after Moses. To anticipate, the *Asclepius*, and all the other texts forming the *Corpus Hermeticum* were composed just before Lactantius and Augustine read them, between AD 100 and 300, in the ambience of contemporary Gnosticism, Platonism and Stoic philosophy, with some Jewish and perhaps Persian contributions. But they were firmly believed in by medieval scholars: in the twelfth century Hermes Triplex was ranked with Enoch and Moses as king, philosopher and prophet, and Roger Bacon thought Hermes 'Father of Philosophers'. In fifteenth-century Italy Marsilio Ficino translated the Greek Hermetic *Corpus* into Latin in 1463, and thenceforward the belief in a pre-Platonic *prisca theologia* behind all learning, and as old as, or older than Moses, became an important component in all thinking about antiquity. For if Hermes was really Thoth and taught the ancient Egyptians, the Christian tradition going back to Stephen, Saint and Protomartyr, was that 'Moses was learned in all the wisdom of the Egyptians' (Acts 7:22). The true date of the Hermetic texts was in fact demonstrated, with fine humanistic scholarship, by Isaac Casaubon in his Protestant riposte to the Counter-Reformation world history of Cesare Baronio, in 1614, but many scholars and antiquaries ignored this and continued to champion Hermes. Sir Walter Raleigh, publishing his *History of the World* in 1614 and therefore ignorant of Casaubon, quotes in his Preface 'Hermes, who lived at once with, or soon after, Moses' and ranks him with 'those enititled by St Augustine, *summi philosophi*, philosophers of highest judgment and understanding' (Bk I Chap.ii). John Everard, editing an Hermetic text in 1649, confidently dated Hermes 'some hundreds of years' before Moses; Sir Thomas Browne in his *Religio Medici* of 1643 delighted in Hermes and vowed that 'the severe Schools shall never laugh me out of the Hermetical Philosophers'; a century later Stukeley was treating the Hermetic tradition with respect, and Newton had thought that the true knowledge of the universe had been revealed by God to the *prisci theologi* of the Hermetic philosophers.

Despite what Frances Yates describes as this 'huge historical error', the authority and antiquity of the Pentateuch and its author were dangerously called into question by Hermes and the Egyptians, and the desire to establish on a firm base the seniority of Moses certainly sharpened the intensity of research into Biblical chronology. This was complementary to the availability of printed vernacular texts of the Old and New Testaments, and the importance attached particularly in English Puritanism, to personal interpretation based on a minute and literal reading of the text. This could now be taken up by any literate person in the English versions culminating in that of 1611; the better educated could add the Latin Vulgate, and the learned divine could tackle the original Greek and Hebrew. The application of these methods of exegesis to the text of the Pentateuch, and especially the Book of Genesis, was to provide the background into all investigation into early man, and for the English antiquaries, the setting for the ancient Briton. It was also to reveal some unexpected difficulties and sometimes to suggest alarming conclusions. 'And truly', Sir Thomas Browne wrote, 'for the first chapters of Genesis, I must confess a great deal of obscurity' and he was not alone in his perplexity.

The Pentateuch, as we see it today in the light of modern Biblical criticism, is a Jewish priestly compilation hardly earlier than the fifth century BC, and containing a collection of origin and aetiological myths, legendary genealogies and history, traditional legal codes, hero-tales and wisdom literature; some material may have its origins as early as the ninth century BC and all of it likely to have resulted from oral rather than written tradition, though Early Hebrew literacy goes back to the eleventh century BC. The text of Genesis where it particularly concerns us embodies two early versions of the Creation myth, the E and J texts (from the use of *Elohim* and *Yahweh* respectively for the Deity); a later Priestly recension accounts for much of the rest. In general the Pentateuch, with the rest of the Old Testament, is representative of a large body of Near Eastern religious and quasi-historical texts known from much more ancient sources.[8]

The Genesis narrative which concerned the early antiquaries was that which described the Creation; the subsequent population of the world by its flora and fauna culminating in Man (Gen 1,2); the Original Sin and the expulsion of Adam and Eve from Eden (Gen 3); and the subsequent degeneracy of mankind (Gen 4), culminating in the alternative pedigrees from Seth consisting of fabulous patriarchs ending in Lamech, who sired Noah at the age of 182 and lived to be 777. Now all is set for the story of the Flood and the Ark (Gen 6–8) with the emergence of Noah, his wife and married sons, to people the post-Diluvial world (Gen 10), with Japhet responsible for Europe and the west. On Ussher's chronology, with the Creation at 4004 BC, the Flood occurred in 2448 BC, less than 2,000 years later and 4,000 years before the present. To the modern mind, accustomed to thinking in millennia and of man as a species whose ancestors evolved 2½ million years ago, this has seemed a ludicrously inadequate time-span, but to the sixteenth and seventeenth centuries it seemed very long. With an expectation of life of only thirty years even among the nobility, a century was a long time; the last 2,000 years had seen a world change from classical antiquity to Christianity and the Middle Ages and the Renaissance with its new and momentous inventions of gunpowder, the mariner's compass and the printing press, and an equal antecedent period could surely embrace the development of early man from the time his ancestors stepped out of the Ark. It was widely thought that the descendants of Japhet had taken no more than two or three centuries to reach Britain, and would certainly have been settled there before 2000 BC. As it happens the earliest antiquities recognized by the first antiquaries in the field, the Neolithic long barrows of Wessex, could, before the application of radiocarbon dating in the 1950s, still be accommodated within a Neolithic period beginning *c*. 2000 BC by modern archaeologists, including the present writer.[9]

Genesis and mankind

We may now turn to the ways in which a literal reading of Genesis contributed, consciously or unconsciously, to the picture of the past formed by the educated world of the Elizabethans and Stuarts so far as it applied to man's primitive state. In a providential world, with Man, his Fall and Redemption as the climax of a purposive plan, the earth with its plants and animals, the seas with their fishes and the fowls of the air, were created as a direct contribution to his well-being. In the E text creation account (in which Adam is not mentioned) newly created man is given 'dominion over the fish of the sea, and over the fowl of the air, and over the cattle, and over all the earth, and over every creeping thing that creepeth upon the earth'; later vegetation is added – 'every herb bearing seed, which is upon the face of the earth, and every tree, which is the fruit of a tree-bearing seed, to you it shall be for meat' (Gen 1:26, 29–30). Keith Thomas has set out in sympathetic detail the reaction to this 'breathtakingly anthropocentric spirit in which Tudor and Stuart preachers interpreted the biblical story'[10] and which was central to views of early man and the exploitation of plants and animals. One point which does not seem to have been made is the concept of the relationship between wild and domesticated animals, and of both to man, held by the original redactors of the Genesis texts, their translators, and their commentators seeking a picture of the cultural status of the first men.

The propensity of early writers (and illustrators) to project the modern into the ancient world without any sense of what came to be known as anachronism, is a commonplace. Medieval drawings of Biblical scenes are a valuable source for the material culture of the European Middle Ages but not of that of the ancient Levant; the Tower of Babel is being built with the full technological equipment of the master mason of cathedral or castle, and Pharaoh's vehicle sent to bring Jacob and his family back to Egypt can be a coach of fourteenth-century high fashion.[11] In such a climate of thought, which was to endure well beyond the Middle Ages, a world in which man existed without the familiar farmyard domesticated animals was difficult to imagine, and when encountered among the American Indians, was explained as part of the general degeneracy incident to the Fall and remoteness from the original fount of civility. Certainly the modern archaeologists' concept of domestic animals and plants as technological artifacts, with an appreciation of the complex and long-term variables of association in animal management leading to eventual domestication, were unknown in the past and are indeed a part of recent developments in archaeology, zoology and botany over the last few decades.[12] Small wonder then that the Genesis narrative reflects the ancient assumptions, and its later interpretation only confirmed them.

In the Authorized Version careful and consistent distinction is made between 'beasts' and 'cattle' from the first moment of Creation: 'And God made the beasts of the earth after his kind, and the cattle after their kind' (Gen 1:25), reflecting the Vulgate *bestias* and *jumenta*, where Jerome uses the unambiguous word for a draught animal. This was normal Elizabethan usage: Arthur Golding translating Pomponius Mela in 1590 writes of 'Cattell and wilde Beastes' with cattle as property in flocks and herds.[13] Other comparable phrases continue, but when the animals enter the Ark (Gen 7:14) they begin with 'every beast after his kind, and all the cattle after their kind'. This might be taken as domestication between the Fall and the Flood, but the first quotation is decisive, as is the distinction again made between 'cattle' and 'every beast' when Adam is naming the animals (Gen 2:20). The distinction is present in the Hebrew and Septuagint texts, and there seems no doubt that from the compilation of the Pentateuch up to its interpretation by the divines and antiquaries of the sixteenth and seventeenth centuries it was accepted that domesticated animals were a part of the original Creation, and present for the use of man from the first. They then entered the Ark with him, and were there to accompany him on at least the first stages of the dispersal of the progeny of Noah.

It was also generally accepted that, like Adam and Eve, all animals were vegetarian and pacific, on the authority of Gen 1:30, 'And to every beast of the earth . . . I have given every green herb for meat.' The Old Testament prophets too had looked forward to an eventual renewal of Paradise in which 'the wolf also shall dwell with the lamb, and the leopard shall lie down with the kid . . . and the lion shall eat straw like the ox' (Isaiah 11:6–7). After the publication in 1667 of *Paradise Lost*, Milton's majestic poem did much to influence Englishmen in their ideas of Eden, and here for the delectation of Adam and Eve the animals played, and even Jumbo did his circus tricks

> Sporting the Lion rampd, and in his paw
> Dandl'd the Kid: Bears, Tygers, Ounces, Pards
> Gambold before them, th'unwieldy Elephant
> To make them mirth us'd all his might, & wreathed
> His Lithe Proboscis.

> (*Paradise Lost* IV, 340–44)

The question arose again however when after the Fall the animals entered the Ark: had they by then suffered the general curse of God and turned carnivorous, and if so, what provision did Noah make for their feeding; alternatively did they become temporary vegetarians for the duration, to return to their lapsed state on emergence? Such problems were discussed with great seriousness, as we shall see in the next chapter.

Preadamites

But worse could result from the literal reading of Genesis. In 1655 a Bordeaux Calvinist, Isaac de Lapeyrère, published in Latin his *Systema Theologicum ex Praeadamitarum Hypothesi: Prae-adamitae*, and the next year an English translation, *Man Before Adam*, appeared. In a discourse on Original Sin he made use of the two unreconciled versions of the Creation, the E text of Gen 1 and the J text of Gen 2, only the second of which names Adam and Eve, and proposed that the E text should be taken to mean that a separate and large population of Preadamites was created before Adam, who was merely the progenitor of the Jews, not of all mankind. This Gentile, non-Adamic, non-Jewish past was of vast antiquity, as was the fund of wisdom and knowledge acquired over this long period. The Flood, as an episode in Jewish ancient history, need only have been limited in extent, and far distant regions such as the Americas could have been populated by Preadamites in a remote antiquity.[14]

Not surprisingly, Lapeyrère's views caused something of a sensation. There was immediate reaction: refutations poured from the pens of Grotius and many lesser scholars on the Continent; the bishop of Namur condemned Lapeyrère for heresy and in England the *Prae-Adamitae* seems to have prompted Sir Matthew Hale's widely read book, the *Primitive Origination of Mankind* (1677). It obviously raised a number of awkward questions, about the universality of the Flood and not least in reference to ancient non-Mosaic wisdom, which immediately gave a new lease of life to Hermes Trismegistus, who despite Isaac Casaubon, was in England enjoying renewed popularity among the Neoplatonists, and with the position of Moses as the most ancient author again under suspicion, the chronologists were on their guard. Concern with historical peoples outside the classical and biblical field such as Egyptians took on a new life. Interest in Egypt and its ancient wisdom had of course existed as early as Herodotus, and was revived in the Italian Renaissance with the publication of historical fragments such as those of the Egyptian priest Manetho and the Babylonian Berosus contained in the *Contra Apionem* of Josephus (Latin translation 1480, first published 1544) and critically edited by J.J. Scaliger in his *Thesaurus Temporum* of 1606. The MS of the Greek text of Horapollo, probably fifth-century AD and purporting to be by an ancient Egyptian, was in Florence about 1420 and was published by Aldus in 1505, with a Latin translation in 1515. The reliefs and hieroglyphic inscriptions on the many surviving Egyptian monuments naturally presented a challenge, and the fact that no Egyptian script could be read until Champollion's pioneer decipherment in the early nineteenth century proved less a deterrent than an encouragement to interpreters of their meaning. The indefatigable Jesuit polymath, Athanasius Kircher, sure in advance that the inscriptions contained 'the esoteric knowledge of the Egyptians', with the aid of the classical authors, Hermetic Neoplatonism, the Jewish Cabala and the Christian

Fathers, published no less than six volumes of some 3,000 folio pages on this theme between 1636 and 1666.[15] Misleading and erroneous though it all was, this literature did provide the British antiquary with an historical view widened beyond the Bible and the classics, and was to have considerable influence on the picture of the ancient Briton and his ancestry which for instance Aylett Sammes and William Stukeley presented to their readers.

The discussion provoked by the Preadamites also aroused interest in the question of the cultural status of mankind before and immediately after the Fall, of importance to antiquaries when considering that of the first inhabitants of Europe and Britain. Degeneration had certainly taken place in the westward trek from Ararat, but from what degree of civilization, and where did the Preadamites come in? A reading of Gen 4 and the aetiological myth of the origin of the divergent economies of pastoralism and agriculture in the story of Abel and Cain ('And Abel was a keeper of sheep but Cain was a tiller of the ground'; Gen 4:2) suggested to Lapeyrère and many others that when the banished Cain 'builded a city' and became the father of Jubal and Tubal, respectively the inventors of musical instruments and of metal-working (Gen 4:17–22), he was in a context of quite complex technology. The whole picture then would be a state of culture which possessed domesticated draught and herd animals; plough agriculture with cereal crops; architectural and allied skills; metal-working and music – all attributable to Preadamites, said Lapeyrère – and a fair summary in fact of ancient and medieval technology to which could be added, with Noah, ship-building and navigation, and indeed viticulture. With such an array of practical skills, it was difficult to think of their total loss in the post-Diluvial westward colonization, however powerful the effect of degeneration. Here was to be a rich field for antiquarian speculation.

Jubal and Tubal as 'inventors' introduce an explanatory process in the early discussions of the history of technology which was to be regarded as entirely satisfactory from early antiquity until as late as eighteenth-century England. If a piece of technology of unknown antiquity were provided with a named mythical inventor, no more need be said: the problem was solved. So Tubal or Vulcan for metallurgy, Cadmus or Thoth for writing: Triptolemus and Ceres as the inventors of plough agriculture with cereals were not only the poetic fictions of the writer Callimachus in the third century BC but were commemorated in the chronological inscription of the 'Parian Marble' of the same date. In the Renaissance the acute scholar

Polydore Vergil published his *De inventoribus rerum* in 1439 and 1521: it was translated into English in 1546 and was immensely successful, setting forth 'who invented or began all things or arts ... who first did anything splendid or unusual'. And in 1699 Dr John Woodward, in controversy with John Edwards of Cambridge, wrote a learned dissertation, entirely from such literary sources, to demonstrate that there was no agriculture among the inhabitants of ancient Europe until Triptolemus.[16]

Ancient giants

One incidental and curious outcome of this exploration of the dark corners of the Pentateuch was to have a surprisingly long life and vitality among antiquaries up to the nineteenth century, and that was the belief in giants among the ancient population both before and after the Flood. Giants had of course been a part of international myth and folklore since early antiquity, and had taken different forms, like bad individual ogre-giants such as Polyphemus or Fee-fi-fo-fum, or sociable and well-meaning giants who could be aboriginal, and club-bearing and shaggy, become the Wild Men and Woodwoses of medieval Europe.[17] In popular fancy giants had been the obvious builders of megalithic monuments, from the *tombe di giganti* of the Mediterranean, by way of *tombeaux des géants*, *Riesengräber* and *jaettestuer* to the Baltic, with Stonehenge as *Chorea Gigantum*. But we have also to deal with giants as part and subject of learned antiquarian debate, and part of the Preadamite unorthodoxy.

The references to giants in the Old Testament were obscure and mysterious, which made them, of course, all the more fascinating to the commentators. In Gen 6:4 we have, 'There were giants in the earth in those days; and also after that, when the sons of God came in unto the daughters of men, and they bare children to them, the same became mighty men of old, men of renown.' Here we have the familiar degeneracy theme, in which the heroes of antiquity not only possessed superior wisdom, longevity and procreative power (like Methusalah siring Lamech at the age of 187 and dying at 969; Lamech following with Noah produced when he was 182 and living to be 777). These were indeed mighty men of renown, and should have had appropriate superior stature. The well-worn trope of moderns as dwarfs standing on the shoulders of giants, going back to the twelfth century, was much in use in seventeenth-century England, and for some it certainly had a literal sense. Biblical giants again appear, even more mysterious, in

Numbers 13:33, 'And there we saw the giants, the sons of Anak, which come of the giants: and we were in our sight as grasshoppers, and so were we in their sight.' These, said Lapeyrère, were Preadamite giants, who with the rest colonized far and wide before the children of Noah. And by the Middle Ages Gog and Magog (Cf. Ezekiel 38) had changed from northern tribes to giants, or a composite Gogmagog.

The medieval world-picture easily accommodated primeval giants in England attested by huge bones, perhaps those of mammoths: Ralph of Coggeshall described giant's bones from the Essex coast in the thirteenth century, and others were subsequently recorded from the Yorkshire coast and from Bardney near Lincoln.[18] Giants played important parts in the medieval story of the legendary peopling of Britain offered by Geoffrey of Monmouth in the twelfth century, and enthusiastically championed in the sixteenth century by John Bale, John Twyne and Richard White. 'The island was then called Albion and was inhabited by none but a few giants', as Aaron Thompson translated Geoffrey in 1718, and when Brutus and his companion Corineus arrived, the latter killed a 'detestable monster, named Goëmagog, in stature twelve cubits' at Plymouth, where a turf-cut figure or figures of the giant was being cleaned by 1486 and survived until at least 1602; near Cambridge the Gogmagog Hills, first mentioned in 1640, may preserve the memory of another hill-figure of a giant.[19] Sir Thomas Kendrick has detailed the fascinating elaborations of the Geoffrey of Monmouth legendary British History concocted by its supporters in the sixteenth century,[20] and all include giants as historical characters. John Bale, Bishop of Ossory, in his *Illustrium majoris Britanniae scriptorum . . .* (1548) has Albion King of Britain, a wicked giant descended from Noah through Ham, who died in 1708 BC; Richard White, publishing between 1597 and 1607 his massive *Historiarum Britanniae*, has British giants from the line of Cain and Enoch (Gen 4:17) arriving here in pre-Diluvial times (and so anticipating Lapeyrère's Preadamites); John Twyne (*De Rebus Albionicis . . .* published posthumously in 1590 and incidentally used as a source by Sir Thomas Browne) again has Albion and a race of giants arriving before the Flood, who built megalithic monuments. Nearly a century later a Dutch antiquary, Johan Picardt, in his *Korte Beschryvinge van . . . Antiquiteten* (1660) enthusiastically presented giants as the builders of the megalithic tombs of Drenthe before the Flood, quoting Gen 6:4 and illustrating them at work (and making a snack of some puny humans) in rousing and realistic engravings. In England Sir Thomas Elyot, in his Latin–English dictionary of 1538 under *gigas* recorded

how about eight years before they had 'at a monastery of regular canons, called Juy Churche, two miles from the citie of Sarisbury' discovered the 'body of a deade man founde deep in the grounde, when they dygged stones . . . in length xiiii feet and ten ynches.' This giant was to be frequently quoted, moving from 'near Salisbury' to 'near Stonehenge' to 'at Stonehenge', where he was to be appealed to by Lord Monboddo, the Scottish philosopher, in his *Ancient Metaphysics* (1779–99), in the context also of the building of German and Danish

1 Ancient Dutch giants and the megalithic tomb they have built, engraving from Johan Picardt's Korte beschryvinge van . . . Antiquiteten *(1660).*

megalithic monuments, as a striking example of the present degeneracy of mankind.[21] Small wonder then that Dr Plot in his *Enquiries* of 1678–79 should ask, 'Are there any ancient *Sepulchres* hereabout of Men of *Gigantick Stature, Roman Generals* or *others* of ancient times?'[22] Giants were to be expected in English field archaeology.

And an amusing postscript comes from a late eighteenth-century antiquary, James Douglas (1752–1819), who was one of the first to recognize pagan Saxon antiquities for what they were. Every modern archaeologist who has excavated extended inhumation burials knows how the public invariably regard them as abnormally tall. Douglas was excavating Saxon inhumations with navvy labour from the military during the making of the Chatham Lines in Kent, when 'on the opening of a barrow, I was hurried from my repast . . . by three Irish soldiers . . . with the assurance that they had discovered a perfect skeleton, the enormous size of which they pronounced, before I reached the spot, to have been the carcass of a prodigious giant.' It was of course a perfectly normal burial, but the infuriated Douglas 'seized a thigh-bone from the grave, and having made one fellow stand erect to measure it by his own, I belaboured the fellow with it . . . It cured my spleen and I returned in better humour.'[23]

From the Creation to the Flood, whatever the chronology, the early antiquaries of Tudor, Stuart and early Hanoverian England could base their knowledge of the earliest mankind on what appeared to be and was universally accepted as an impeccable historical text: the Pentateuch written by Moses. It might have its difficulties, its ambiguities, and even at times its apparent contradictions, but it retained its ultimate authority. But once the events narrated in Gen 10 had taken place, the story of the descendants of Noah, apart from those ancestral to the Jews, was unsupported by any historical texts until, in Europe, classical writers, themselves with no more than mythical ancestors, commented on Germans, Gauls or Britons. Nothing but inference, supposition or sheer imagination could give an account of the long journey westwards from Ararat – from 'Shinaar to Biscay', Sir Walter Raleigh reckoned in *History of the World* of 1614, was a matter of 69 degrees of longitude and so 4140 miles. In this hazardous, but for the early history of western man fundamental enquiry, the early antiquaries had two options, a pessimistic and an optimistic view of what was thought to have taken place. These will be discussed in more detail in the next chapter but may be briefly stated here. The pessimistic history was the one strictly in accordance with orthodox Christian theology and more immediately with that of the Reformed churches, with stress on the Fall with its original act of Sin, the subsequent persistence in ways unacceptable to God provoking the retributive act of the Flood, and the migration of sinful and degenerate mankind over an inhospitable earth to await spiritual redemption in the terms set out in the New Testament. The ancient Europeans and Britons by inference, and soon the American Indians by observation and experience, were the degraded remnants, the wretched end products, of a long history of divine wrath.

The optimistic view was given a degree of expression in the concept of the Preadamites, with whom went the supposition of a partial deluge and so of parts of the world perhaps spared from the awful visitations of Yahweh upon the territorially restricted Jewish people. With this could easily be assimilated the repositories of ancient wisdom outside the Genesis narrative but embodied in thrice-great Hermes and the other Gentile magi and seers, which from the time of the Church Fathers came to include Zoroaster, Indian Gymnosophists and Druids. Samuel Bochart, Aylett Sammes and William Stukeley were to be the protagonists of an optimistic picture of the peopling of Europe and Britain in which the Phoenicians, first introduced by Twyne (of the Albionic giants) in 1590, played an increasingly important part. It was a picture conducive to national self-esteem, and alleviated the inexorable burden of inevitable degeneracy, as did the increasing acceptance of progress in technology, as a part of the Baconian dream, the triumph of the Moderns over the Ancients.

By the early eighteenth century scriptural authority was waning under the influence of Deism and Latitudinarianism in the Anglican church, the influence that Stukeley set out to combat. Geologists and others were extending the permissible time-scale: as early as 1738 the geologist Thomas Story, examining the stratification of the cliffs at Scarborough, concluded that the earth was 'of much older date than the time assigned in the Holy Scriptures';[24] by mid-century Rousseau, writing of primitive man after the Flood, could talk airily of 'infinite time' and 'thousands of centuries' involved in his subsequent development; in 1797 John Frere would assign the palaeolithic hand-axes of Hoxne 'to a very remote period indeed, even beyond that of the present world'.[25] And the ordinary literate man in the street could enjoy the joke when William King in 1776 wrote in jolly Chestertonian verse of those who declared

> That all the books of Moses
> Were nothing but supposes . . .
> That as for Father Adam
> And Mistress Eve, his Madam
> And what the Devil spoke, Sir
> Twas nothing but a joke, Sir
> And well invented flam.[26]

3
From the Ark to the Americas

For the early antiquaries the last and in many ways the most important point of dependence on scriptural authority was the account of the Flood, the building and cargo of the Ark, and the subsequent peopling of the West by the sons of Noah. For here should be found our earliest ancestors, the most ancient Britons, inevitably of Noachian ancestry whether seen in the prevalently pessimistic or occasionally optimistic schemes outlined in the last chapter, and with them not only their domesticated animals but the wild beasts, the birds of the air and the fish of the seas, together with the trees and grass, the herbs and weeds, combining to form the background of a restored post-Diluvial Nature in which mankind had to establish himself anew. What went into the Ark had to come out of it, and the terse statements in Gen 6–8 presented a challenge to the subtle exegete intent on detecting every detail of divine intention and performance.

The Biblical literalness of the Puritans was no doubt often excessive and obsessive, but rarely compares with that applied to the Ark by the Counter-Reformation scholar, Fr Athanasius Kircher SJ. In his *Arca Noe in tres libris digesta* . . . (Amsterdam 1675) he brings to bear, in text and engravings, an exact devotion to the words of Genesis coupled with a sort of crazy common sense. There was the question of the exact species of animal to be included, for instance: obviously those named by Adam (Gen 2:19), but which were these, and did they perhaps include some regarded mythical? On a review of the evidence Kircher reduced these to three; the mermaid (and presumably a merman), the gryphon (best known to us from another work of fiction, *Alice in Wonderland*) and the unicorn, already included by the poet Michael Drayton (1563–1631) who hinted that he had temporarily to keep low company –

> The Unicorne leaves off his pride, and closse
> There sets him downe by the Rhinoceros.

Kircher's reptiles went into the bilge and insects were not included as these generated spontaneously; if it proved that some beasts remained carnivorous, an extra percentage of sheep and goats must be allowed for, and in any case the problem of mucking out the stalls had to be taken seriously and their size worked out proportionately to their occupants, from elephants to mice. Noah was instructed to bring 'food for thee and for them' (Gen 6:21) and there it is in Kircher's drawing, neatly stowed in sacks and casks; querns were included to make flour for the family. He thought of everything and doubtless believed God had done just the same.[1]

Kircher's deservedly popular book, with its wonderful illustrations, merely exemplifies the general state of belief about the Ark and its animals, an irresistible fairy-story, still today part of the child's toy cupboard. But the animal population of pre-Diluvian times was a serious matter of discussion, quite apart from mermaids and gryphons. To us today, inordinate importance was attached, from the early days of the Church, to the act of Adam at God's command, naming the animals (Gen 2:19), for it was commonly held in the sixteenth and seventeenth centuries that in doing so, Adam shared and expressed God's wisdom, because to know the name was to know the 'real' or ideal qualities of a lion or a lamb. It was then no mere exercise in pre-Linnean taxonomy, but the possession of a magic secret, a word of power. 'The savage commonly fancies', wrote Sir James Frazer, 'that the link between a name and the person denominated by it is not a mere arbitrary and ideal association, but a real and substantial bond which unites the two.'[2] An un-named animal could not exist, as it was not recognized by God. The naming by Adam did not include fish, as Milton noticed and was quick with a matter-of-fact reason given by the Deity

> I bring them to receave
> From thee thir Names, and pay thee fealtie
> With low subjection; understand the same
> Of Fish within thir watry residence
> Not hither summond, since they cannot change
> Thir Element to draw the thinner Aire.[3]

But the Preadamite supporters had further doubts about the animals of the New World, as to whether they were divinely transported to Adam for naming, and then quickly returned to their native habitat. However, of the importance of the event there was no doubt, and scholars such as Samuel Bochart stressed this, not only in his

Geographia Sacra (1646–7) but in *Hierozoicon* (1663), demonstrating the naming to have been in Hebrew. The Hermetic Neoplatonists had been assimilating the ideas of magic names, including the Magic Names of God, from the Hebrew Cabala, and in the 1660s Leibniz was concerned with the *lingua Adamica* as a magic language in which he seems to have believed.[4] The secret Name of Power survives in modern international folktale as the Rumpelstiltskin motif, and the belief in Hebrew as the language of Adam, Noah and his descendants, and so ultimately of early Britain, was widespread among the early antiquaries. The old fantasies had remarkable staying power. The parson–antiquary Samuel Lysons vigorously supported Hebrew as the language of the Ancient Britons in *Our British Ancestors: Who and What Were They?* of 1865; in 1872 a paper was read to the Anthropological Institute, with Sir John Lubbock in the chair, by C. Staniland Wake on Adamites and pre-Adamites.[5]

The world after the Flood

On the retreat of the waters after the Flood and the Ark grounded on Ararat, the progenitors of mankind emerged into a world of which the Genesis narrative offers no description but which was of obvious concern to the early commentators as the terrain over which Noah's progeny, and for British antiquaries especially those of Japhet, were to make their dispersal. The question of vegetation – pasture for cattle, forests for wild beasts – was an insistent one, and speculation alone could decide. Genesis shows little interest in the vegetable creation except as fodder for flocks and herds – it embodies after all the ancient Hebrew pastoralists' charter. The flood was to destroy man, cattle, fowls and creeping things (Gen 7:23) but no mention is made of the plant cover. For those of the Preadamite persuasion, a localized flood allowed of vast unsubmerged areas; for the others, those favouring a disastrous cataclysm ignored the problem, while for many a gentle inundation (lasting exactly 365 days, Kircher calculated) could allow of survival, with great play being made of the dove returning with the olive leaf (Gen 8:9–12).[6] Sir Walter Raleigh in 1614 saw the situation in the practical light of personal experience:

First, therefore, we must call to mind and consider, what manner of face the earth every where had in the 130th year after the great inundation . . . what wonderful deserts, what impassible fastnesses of woods, reeds, briers, and rotten grass, what lakes, and standing pools, and what marshes, fens and bogs, all the face of the earth (excepting the mountains) were pestered withal.

Writing in his imprisonment in the Tower, he was here surely recalling the 'broken islands and drowned lands', the 'woods, bushes, prickles and thorns' of his own Virginia and Guiana expeditions. He goes on to stress the difficulties posed 'for a nation or family of men, with their wives and children, and cattle, to travel 3,000 miles through woods, bogs and desarts . . . For, in the West Indies, of which the Spaniards have the experience, in those places where they found neither path nor guide, they have not entered the country ten miles in ten years.'[7]

After an arduous journey through such a landscape (Raleigh, knowing all too well the hazards of even Elizabethan seamanship, dismissed the possibility of ancient navigation, as did others), for British antiquaries there was then the problem of the last move of the first inhabitants into an island, for the question of the pre-diluvial existence or the post-diluvial formation of a recognizable modern coast-line was a matter of debate. The Americas posed this problem in its most acute form, but our concern is with the British Isles. George Owen, in his manuscript *Description of Pembrokeshire in General* of 1603 saw them as the result of

the violence of the generall floode, which at the departure thereof breake southward and tare the erthe in peeces and separated the Ilands from the Contynent, and made the hills and valleies as we now finde them.[8]

Many took the same view and used a disruptive deluge to account for fossil shells in elevated positions, but for others there was the alternative of a partial and localized Flood, an idea we have seen associated with the Preadamites. Dr Plot, writing in 1667, firmly took up this position. Fossils, he said, were brought to their present location

not by the Flood in the days of *Noah*, because that (and for very good reasons too) seems not to have been *universal*, and at most to have covered only the *Continent* of *Asia*, and not to have extended it self to this then uninhabited Western part of the World.[9]

In support, he quoted Edward Stillingfleet, *Origines Sacrae* (1662), and the view was shared by Isaac Vossius (who liked being unorthodox) and Georg Kirchmaier in 1667.[10] Camden had toyed with the idea of a recent insulation of Britain, but we may recall how Aylett Sammes in 1676 indignantly repudiated the idea on patriotic grounds.

An argument for an English Channel land-bridge was put up by an antiquary who was mainly concerned with the Anglo-Saxons in Britain, Richard Verstegen, whose *Restitution of Decayed Intelligence in Antiquities . . .* was published in Antwerp in 1605, and significantly reprinted in London in 1673, in the favourable atmosphere of Restoration antiquarianism. Verstegen was of a Dutch Catholic family which came to England about 1500 and took the name of Rowlands, and, as Richard Rowlands, was at Christ Church in 1565, where he studied history and Anglo-Saxon. His religion caused him to return to Antwerp and resume his original family name in Elizabeth's reign: he became friendly with another Catholic exile, Richard White, who was as we saw in the last chapter an old-fashioned adherent to the Geoffrey of Monmouth legendary history. Verstegen was fervently Anglophile, and as a Dutchman had first-hand knowledge of land submergence, and his lively and engaging little book has an engraving of fossils which is probably the earliest in an English language publication.

He put up a sound case for a land-bridge 'where our Country was then no Island but Peninsula, being thus fixed unto the main continent of the World', and supported its post-diluvial survival by an ingenious argument –

the Patriarch *Noe* having had with him in the *Ark* all sorts of beasts . . . these then after the flood being put forth of the *Ark* to increase and multiply, did afterward in time disperse themselves over all parts of the continent or main land, but long after it could not be before the ravenous Wolf had made his kind nature known unto man, and therefore no man unless he were mad would ever transport of that race for the goodness of the breed, out of the continent into any Isles.

Wolves were topical in 1605, for their recent extermination in England and Wales was, as Keith Thomas has said, 'a matter of some importance and the occasion of much self-congratulation' in Tudor England: they survived until the late seventeenth century in Scotland and the mid eighteenth in Ireland.[11] The problem was later seen with regard to the Americas, where Justus Lipsius in 1637 thought rattlesnakes would never have been taken by colonists in boats and Abraham Milius in 1667 said the same of lions, tigers, bears, snakes and dragons.[12]

The patristic and medieval view of the dispersal of mankind after the Flood had been a version of the pessimistic degeneration scheme, with Paradise in the east, the final extinction to be in the west. In the early twelfth century Hugh of St Victor wrote his *De Arca Noë morali* and *De Arca Noë mystica*, demonstrating that the earliest post-Diluvial kingdoms of the Assyrians, Chaldeans and Medes lay to the east, and the seat of empire had now moved westward to Rome, where the end of the world would take place.[13] In the same mood some would later point to the woeful degeneracy of the ancient Gauls, Germans and

Britons as revealed by the classical writers such as Caesar or Tacitus made available in the Renaissance. Sir Thomas Browne in 1646 pointed out that, 'Learning, Civility and Arts have their beginning in the East' but 'travelled late and slowly into our *quarters* ... he that shall peruse the work of *Tacitus de moribus Germanorum* may easily discern how little civility two thousand years had wrought upon that Nation', and Strabo confirmed this for Britain, 'to the dishonour of our *Predecessors*, and the disparagement of those who glory in the antiquity of their Ancestors'.[14] The discovery of the New World Indians and Eskimos reinforced this gloomy view, and although Bishop Berkeley wrote his famous lines on the medieval theme –

> Westwards the course of empire takes its way
> The first four acts already past –

and visited America in 1728 in an optimistic spirit, there is no doubt that the general feeling was that west was worse.

But at least the benighted barbarians of the west had respectable ancestors. Their ultimate link with Adam and the patriarchs was recorded in Gen 10:1–5, where Noah's sons and grandsons are enumerated: the sons of Japhet and of his sons including Gomer and Javan. 'By these were the isles of the Gentiles divided in their lands', *divisae sunt insulae gentium* (Gen 10:5). The islands of the original fifth-century BC Pentateuch were presumably those of Cyprus, Crete and the Aegean, and Javan conceals the Ionian Greeks, but Gomer was in early modern Europe regarded as the ancestor of all the peoples of the west and some of the English scholars tried to equate the Isles of the Gentiles with the British Isles. The name of Gomer is that of the people who appear in Assyrian records as *Gimirrai* in the eighth century BC, the Greek *Kimmerioi*, the Cimmerians, who had raided Asia Minor in the seventh century BC. But in Tudor and Stuart times Gomer could be equated with the historical Cimbri of Jutland, in Italy with Umbria (Gumbria) and more especially with the Welsh, Cymraeg. As we shall see, by the early eighteenth century, the sons of Gomer were being identified as the Celts. The language they brought with them was of course Hebrew.[15]

In sixteenth-century England there remained one vein of fantastic ancient history to confuse antiquarian thinking, that deriving from Geoffrey of Monmouth's twelfth-century invention, the *Historia Regum Britanniae*. The cherished story of Brutus had been, by the fifteenth century, augmented and given new life by what Kendrick with justice described as 'undoubtedly the most mischievous study of the remote past published during the Renaissance'; a bare-faced literary forgery which was credulously and eagerly accepted from the time of its publication in 1498 until the seventeenth century. A Dominican Abbot of Viterbo, Giovanni Nanni, produced a spurious history of the early peopling of the world allegedly based on Manetho the Egyptian and Berosus the Babylonian (whom we met in Chapter 2): Nanni, who took the Latin name of Annius, invented fictitious texts and commentaries, and published his impudent forgery as *Commentaria super opera diversor . . .* (Rome 1498). The imposture was fully exposed by Gaspar Barreiros in 1565, but by then the damage had been done. Nanni, who became confidential secretary to Pope Alexander VI, was (one feels almost deservedly) poisoned by Alexander's son Cesare Borgia in 1502.

The British history of Geoffrey had in fact been under attack from the early sixteenth century, both of its main figures, Brutus and Arthur, being regarded with suspicion by some English scholars, but the most scathing dismissal was that of Polydore Vergil in his *Anglica Historia* of 1534, made all the worse as coming from an Italian and a Papist. The supporters of Geoffrey like John Bale, Bishop of Ossory, John Caius of Cambridge, and Verstegen's friend, the Catholic emigré John White of Basingstoke, compounded the fantasy of the original by adding the forgeries of Annius, and giving Brutus a detailed pedigree going back to Japhet and Noah, thus making the best of both worlds. Bale and the rest, as we saw, also believed in ancient British giants. The story had become so preposterous that it could not be credited by the new antiquaries: Camden ignored it and it became, as John Speed put it in 1611, 'now universally rejected by all skillfull *Antiquaries*'.[16]

The most ancient Britons

With final removal of the fanciful British History the antiquaries were left with no documentary sources for the ancient Britons save for the legend of Gomer, and once established in Britain, the evidence from the classical sources and the increasing appreciation, from the late fifteenth century, of the use of ethnographical parallels from the Americas and indeed nearer home. But before considering these, it is worth while drawing attention to a linguistic usage of the seventeenth century which reveals the contemporary mental attitude towards the westwards migration from Ararat. From the beginning of the century, the word 'plantation' came into use for the settlements of the English both in Ireland and America, 'involving the transplantation of a section of English society overseas, where it must find a livelihood with aid of cheap land and native labour'[17], and it is hardly surprising that it should be Sir Walter Raleigh in 1614 who wrote, 'Of the first planting of nations after the Flood . . . the world's plantation after the Flood'.[18] Nathanael Carpenter, in his *Geography Delineated forth in two books* (1625) writing of Britain has 'the first plantation of Inhabitants immediately after the Deluge', and Sir Thomas Browne in his *Pseudodoxia* of 1658 'the first plantation of man in those parts'. The usage goes on; Aylett Sammes in *Britannia Antiqua Illustrata* (1676) writes of the 'many pretenders to the first Plantation of a country' and Henry Rowlands, in his *Mona Antiqua Restaurata* (1723) makes it clear that 'Antiquity recordeth, and the consort of Nations celebrateth the sons of *Japhet* to have been the first Planters of *Europe*'. The westward population of Europe from Ararat was then felt to be not wholly a tale of degeneracy, but as the equivalent of the beneficent westward colonization on both sides of the Atlantic by the English, bringing a higher culture to the Wild Irish or American Indian: so the elements of oriental civilization, however attenuated, were planted in Europe and Britain. It is in fact a statement of what became for archaeologists the diffusion hypothesis of the transmission of elements of higher Near Eastern culture westwards into prehistoric Europe, so persuasively put forward by Gordon Childe.

By the later seventeenth century the British antiquaries were coming to form a picture of the ancient Briton which combined a vague view of what constituted savagery in general, supplemented in detail by the observations of the classical writers such as Caesar and Tacitus and, from the 1580s, the use of ethnographical parallels from the Americas and nearer home. Before we come to treat these in the detail they deserve, two general statements may be quoted to set the background of thought about the earliest inhabitants of Britain. The first, though later in time, is perhaps the more representative as the less original and well informed, and was written by the egregious Dr John Woodward, the Dr Fossile of Gay's farce, in 1723

The *Britains* in those Days were barbarous, and wholely unciviliz'd . . . They went naked, and painted their Bodies with the Figures of various Animals, after the Manner of other Savage Nations . . . There was little or nothing that could claim the Name of Science among them. What they had was lodg'd with the Druids, who were the Devines and Philosophers of those Times . . . Nor will it be thought strange that our Progenitors should be, in these early Times, thus rude and unciviliz'd . . . All Mankind all round the Globe were once so, I mean at their first Original, in the Ages that ensu'd after the Deluge.

Woodward went on to say that even the ancestors of the Greeks, those paragons of ancient civilization, 'had no other clothing than only the Skins of Beasts. Some of them dwelt in *Caves*, others in mean *Hutts*, others ran wild in the *Woods* . . . They lived upon *Leaves* and *Herbs*, or upon *Acorns*'.[19]

A far more acute intelligence had been brought to bear on the subject by John Aubrey, writing of North Wiltshire about 1659. The natural condition of the landscape would be that of

a shady dismal wood: and the inhabitants as savage as the beasts whose skins were their only rayment. The language British, which for the honour of it was in those dayes spoken from the Orcades to Italie and Spain. The boats on the Avon (which signifies River) were basketts of twigges covered with an oxe skin: which the poor people of Wales use to this day. They call them *curricles*. Within this shire I believe there were several *Reguli* which often made war upon another: and the great ditches which run on the plaines and elsewhere so many miles (not unlikely) their boundaries: and withall served for defence against the incursions of their enemies . . . Their religion is at large described by Caesar. Their priests were Druids. Some of their temples I pretend to have restored, as Avebury, Stonehenge, &c, as also British sepulchres. Their waie of fighting is lively sett down by Caesar. Their camps with their way of meeting their antagonists I have sett down in another place. They knew the use of iron. They were 2 or 3 degrees, I suppose, less savage than the Americans.[20]

This contains the essentials of all that was to constitute the first stage in the development of British archaeology: fieldwork on earthworks, barrows and stone circles, the use of the classical texts, the final ethnographic comparison. One point must be remembered, that in the absence of any concept of a long prehistoric time scale, the circumstances of the immediately pre-Roman comments of Caesar or Tacitus could equally well be applied to the earliest inhabitants of Britain. It was a form of anachronism the exact reverse of that whereby early modern geographers happily used classical authors for descriptions of remote modern countries.

Woad, chariots and coracles

From the classical texts, the antiquaries picked up three main items of the ancient Briton's material culture; body paint, chariot warfare and the use of skin-boats. From Caesar's unambiguous sentence – 'all the Britons, without exception, stain themselves with woad, which produces a bluish colouring' (*BG* V.14) – the references to painting or tattooing go on through Pliny, Mela, Martial and Solinus to Herodian in the third and Isidore of Seville in the seventh century AD, where it is

specifically assigned to the Picts. These references were reinforced
when the use of body painting was found among the American Indians
as we shall see, and the painted Picts came to play an important part. In
the meantime, woad-painted Britons became a literary commonplace
up until the nineteenth century:

> A painted herd, they rang'd the Plains and Woods
> And prey'd upon their fellow brutes for food

as Henry Needler wrote in 1728.[21]

Painted naked savages, rather less benighted than the American
Indians, were very much a part of the pessimistic view of man's
westward degeneracy, though Aubrey noted from the classical texts
their iron-working, and how 'their waie of fighting is lively set down by
Caesar'. This would be Celtic chariot warfare, and when in 1676 Aylett
Sammes was inventing a far more optimistic account of the first
peopling of Britain, involving Cimbri from the Black Sea and then
Phoenicians led by the Tyrian Hercules, both arriving before the
Trojan War, he could not resist adding Greeks (continuing the tin
trade), who introduced Homeric chariot warfare. As a result of this
bold invention, Sammes was the first antiquary to have a long
discussion of Celtic chariotry, with the lexical problems of words such
as *covinus* and *essedum*, and a fine illustration of chariot battle in
progress; a subject then hardly touched on until the end of the
eighteenth century (for instance Samuel Pegge in 1795) and modern
times.[22]

Aubrey's reference to skin-covered boats mentioned in the
classical sources and surviving as Welsh coracles opens up a fascinating field, in which the early antiquaries illuminated the prehistoric past
by ethnographical analogies drawn not from remote transatlantic
savages, but from survivals in the British Isles themselves. The ancient
texts describing the use of skinboats in Britain range from Caesar,
Pliny, Lucan and Solinus on to Avienus and Sidonius Appollinaris in
the sixth century A D and thence to medieval sources (such as Giraldus
Cambrensis on their use in Wales in the twelfth century) and the
vernacular texts in Ireland and Wales. In Britain they survive on the
Towy and Teifi rivers today and in the sixteenth century their range
was wider. Camden recorded them in some detail on the Severn in
1586: the fishermen have 'a small thing call'd a *Coracle* . . . of a form
almost oval, made of split Sally-twigs interwoven (round at the
bottom) and on that part next the water cover'd with a horse-hide . . .
so light that coming off the water, they take them upon their backs, and

carry them home.' Camden also describes coracles on the Usk and Wye.[23] Andrew Marvell, in some charming lines written soon after 1650, records the coracle-men on the River Wharfe in Yorkshire near Lord Fairfax's house of Nun Appleton

> And now the *Salmon-Fishers* moist
> Their *Leathern Boats* begin to hoist;
> And like *Antipodes* in shoes,
> Have shod their *Heads* in their *Canoos*.
> How *Tortoise-like*, but not so slow
> These rational *Amphibii* go![24]

But it was Camden who first drew the comparison between ancient and modern. In the section of the *Britannia* 'Ireland and the British Ocean' he wrote, 'But that the Britains used small wicker vessels, cover'd with leather, such as they call *Corraghs* at this day, is evidenced from Pliny, with whom Lucan agrees . . . thus likewise Polyhistor [Solinus].'

Modern usage has 'coracle' for the small river craft manned by one fisherman, and 'curragh' for the skin-covered sea-going boats of the Irish coasts: in both, skin has been replaced by tarred calico in modern times and this curragh survives on the West Irish coast from Mayo to Kerry and the Aran Islands. Sir Walter Raleigh as a young soldier took part in the punitive attack on the papal forces of Smerwick in the Dingle Peninsula in 1580 and remembered what he had seen when writing his *History of the World* in 1614. 'In the time of the Romans', he wrote, 'the Britains had a kind of boat, with which they crossed the seas, made of small twigs, and covered over with leather, of which kind I have seen at the Dingle in Ireland, and elsewhere.' Raleigh was interested in primitive craft, and later, commenting on Isaiah 18:1 went on, 'the boats are . . . of two kinds, either of basket-willow covered with hides (as anciently in Britain) or a tree made hollow in the bottom, and built upon both sides, with canes, of the one sort I have seen in Ireland, of the other in the Indies.'[25] We have seen Aubrey's comments (as a member of a family with South Welsh connections) and it is hardly surprising that in 1723 the Anglesey antiquary Henry Rowlands thought of the first 'planters' of his own island that 'these Men, 'tis most probable, repaired thither, and in their Wicker-*Corrachs* or other expedients of that Time, wafted over to take their primier Possession of Anglesey.'[26] Thereafter, Ancient Britons and coracles became inseparable, as for instance in the delightful aquatint of 'British Fishing and Husbandry' in Meyrick and Smith's picture-book of 1815.[27]

William Camden (1551–
23). Bronze portrait
dallion struck in
mden's memory soon
er his death.

Engraved by C.F. Wigstaff, from a Drawing by Faithorne in the Ashmolean Museum.

JOHN AUBREY.

(Born A.D. 162? Died 1697)

John Aubrey (1626–97). Engraving
om a drawing by William Faithorne
e elder in 1660.

(*right*) Robert Plot (1640–96). Oil
inting by unknown artist of Plot
oking very smug in his Doctor's
wn (DCL 1671, perhaps the date of
e portrait).

4 Edward Lhuyd (1660–1709). Pen
drawing in initial 'E' in the Benefactors
Book of the Ashmolean Museum, Oxford.

5 *(right)* John Toland (1670–1722).
Engraved portrait of 1766, showing him
holding a copy of his philosophical tract
Pantheisticon (1720).

6 *(left)* William Borlase (1695–1772). A
distinguished portrait in oil by Allan
Ramsay, portrait painter to George III
from 1767.

7 *(opposite, above)* William Stukeley
(1687–1765). A bad-tempered self-
portrait in pen and wash made three
years after the completion of his
Stonehenge and Avebury surveys.

8 *(opposite, below left)* William
Cunnington (1754–1810). Engraving from
an oil portrait by Samuel Woodforde,
1808, published as the frontispiece of the
first volume of Hoare's *Ancient Wiltshire*
(1812). Cunnington holds a drawing of
Stonehenge.

9 *(opposite, below right)* Sir Richard
Colt Hoare (1758–1838). Engraving of
pencil and colour portrait by Henry
Edridge, published as the frontispiece of
Ancient Wiltshire, Vol.II (1821). Hoare
correcting proofs of the book, with
Bronze Age pottery from his excavations
on the desk.

THE ARK

10 *(opposite)* Some of the animals entering Noah's Ark, as visualized by Athanasius Kircher in his *Arca Noë* of 1675.

CORACLES

11 *(above)* Sixteenth-century Irish skinboats at Ballyshannon: detail from a large pen and wash drawing of the taking of Enniskillen Castle in 1593 by 'John Thomas solder'.

12 *(left)* Modern Welsh fisherman with his coracle, on the River Towy near Caermarthen.

13 *(below)* A charmingly idyllic pastoral scene of ancient Britons with their coracles; coloured aquatint by Robert Havell 1815.

ESKIMOS, BRITONS AND PICTS

14–18: *(Opposite, above left)* Eskimo brought with his kayak to Bristol by Martin Frobisher in 1576; watercolour drawing by Lucas de Heere. *(Opposite, above right)* Eskimo woman and baby, brought to Bristol by Martin Frobisher in 1577 and seen by William Camden; watercolour drawing by John White. *(Opposite, below left)* Ancient Britons as imagined by Lucas de Heere in a watercolour of 1575, with body paint, long shields and spear from classical sources, and anachronistic sword, and heads of 'wild Irish'. *(Opposite, below right)* A Pict, drawn in watercolour by John White about 1588 from a lost Scottish MS source, in a flamboyant Mannerist style, with body paint, iron torc and waist ring, and head-hunting all from classical sources, and an anachronistic falchion or scimitar. *(Above)* Watercolour by Jacques le Moyne, engraved in 1590 as 'a yonge dowgter of the Pictes' in De Bry's *America*.

A Maeata and *Caledonian*.

C.H.S, del.

Aquatinted by R.Havell.

19 Coloured aquatint by Robert Havell, 1815, of North British tribesmen of the Maeatae and Caledonii, re-worked from the sixteenth-century drawings of 'Picts' (with iron torcs, bulbous spear-butt, falchion-sword etc.), but now in dramatic pose and musculature taken from classical sculpture such as the Laocoön.

The impact of America

After 1492 and the first voyage of Christopher Columbus the world was never to look the same. The impact of America and the American Indians on the European mind is a commonplace, and its effect on the imagination of writers and artists, no less than on the speculations of philosophers and the consciences of Christians, so well known as to be a theme to which little can be added. But one small area of knowledge can be profitably explored, the one directly germane to our present enquiry, the way in which the early antiquaries were influenced in their concept of the ancient Briton by their new knowledge of peoples of a culture which had no European counterparts and was far less sophisticated, technologically and socially, than anything they had previously encountered. We enter the field of ethnographic comparisons in technology, and occasionally of anthropological parallels in social structure, so far as this was understood for peoples on either side of the Atlantic at this time.[28]

We may start with the visual impact of the American Indian in Europe. It is surprising how many captives from across the Atlantic were brought back by the early voyagers: it has been reckoned that between the first voyage of Columbus in 1492 and early in the sixteenth century, at least 1,000 Indians were brought to Europe. In France they were exhibited as striking curiosities in Rouen in 1506, Troyes in 1554, and at a great festival at Bordeaux in 1565. In England, Sebastian Cabot in 1502 brought back three Eskimos in skin garments, eating raw meat, and speaking a strange tongue, who were brought before Henry VII, and William Hawkins in 1532 brought a captured 'Brazilian king' to Henry VIII, 'at the sight of whom the King and all the nobilitie did not a little marvelle . . . All his apparel, behaviour and gesture, were very strange to the beholders'. Contemporary artists began depicting Indians, and as early as 1569 they appear in sculpture on the Harman monument in Burford Church in Oxfordshire, copied from a print by the Flemish artist Cornelis Bos.[29] But from our point of view the most significant encounters were those with the Eskimos abducted from South Baffin Island in 1576 and 1577 by Martin Frobisher, and exibited in Bristol.

On his first voyage to discover the North West Passage, Frobisher forcibly hauled an Eskimo, in his kayak, out of the sea and on to his ship, and brought him back as a trophy to Bristol. On his second voyage in 1577 he captured another man, and a woman with her child, who were likewise brought to England. They appear to have been of the Nugumuit tribe of the Central Eskimo group, and naturally aroused great interest. What is of importance to us is that paintings were made of them, the earliest of such direct records of the natives of the New World, and that they were seen and commented on by no less an English antiquary than William Camden. We must postpone for a moment a fuller discussion of the foreign, and especially Flemish community of artists at this time, but one of them, the distinguished painter Lucas de Heere, the designer of the famous Valois Tapestries, resident in London from 1567 to 1577, came to Bristol and drew the 'Homme sauuage amené de pais Septentrionaux par M. Furbisher L'an 1576'. We shall encounter de Heere again, but returning home in 1577, he did not see Frobisher's captives of that year. They were painted by another Flemish artist, Cornelis Ketel, who was resident in London 1573–81, but these paintings are lost. Fortunately the English artist John White, whose famous watercolour drawings of Indians, made on Raleigh's Virginia expedition of 1585, will shortly concern us, was on Frobisher's 1577 journey and drew the Eskimos then or in Bristol.[30] It is there they must have been seen by the young William Camden, then aged 26, though his published comment was not made until 1615–28, when his Latin *Annals of Great Britain under Queen Elizabeth* was published. Here, in an account of the Frobisher voyages, he writes of the Eskimos 'with black hair, broad faces, flat noses, swarthy coloured, apparelled in sea-calves' skins, the women painted about the eyes and balls of the cheek with a blue colour like the ancient Britons.' White's drawings confirm every detail.[31]

Camden seems to have been the first to make a direct comparison between native American body decoration and that recorded of the ancient Britons, and after Raleigh's Virginia expedition of 1585, and the subsequent publication of John White's drawings in De Bry's *America* of 1590, many people were able to make use of the parallel. But already in 1575 drawings were made of ancient Britons by Lucas de Heere, who as we saw, drew Frobisher's first Eskimo, and must have known Camden. We may pause a moment to consider the colony of foreign artists in London at this time, and start by reminding ourselves that John Smith, in his Latin life of William Camden, described his father as a London *pictor*. Whatever artistic status this implied, young Camden would have been familiar with Flemish painters in London. There was Cornelis Ketel from Gouda, who, as we saw, painted the Frobisher Eskimos, and de Heere, an important figure during his ten years' residence, who was an elder of the Dutch church in Austin Friars and a friend of Emmanuel van Meteren, a cousin of the great geographer Abraham Ortelius who, on his London visit of 1577, persuaded Camden to write the *Britannia*, and was also a friend of Richard Verstegen. Another foreign artist was Jacques Le Moyne de Morgues, a French Huguenot who had been on the abortive Florida expedition and, returning home was wrecked at Swansea in 1565 and lived in London until his death in 1588, when De Bry bought and published his drawings with those of John White.[32]

De Heere is best known to archaeologists from his two surviving books of coloured drawings, both of which include drawings of ancient Britons and one a drawing of Stonehenge, and were executed in *c.* 1573–75.[33] The MS containing the Stonehenge drawing (in the British Library) is a short description (*Corte beschryuinge . . .*) of the British Isles written in Dutch; the other (in the University Library of Ghent) is a costume book of all countries, ancient and modern, with French titles. One of a popular genre of the period – 'from 1560 to 1600 some dozen or more costume books were printed' – it is one of the finest, with 19 pages for the British Isles including ancient and contemporary British and Irish costumes; antique types taken from de Choul, *Discours sur la religion . . .* (1556), an ancient German from Lazius (1557), and the last drawing in the book is Frobisher's Eskimo.[34]

Of the two ancient Briton drawings the pair in the Ghent MS are titled 'Les premiers Anglois comme ils alloyent en guerre du tems du Julius César', and both are closely similar, each with two naked painted men, with shaggy hair and moustaches, bearing long oval shields: in the London drawing one holds a long spear and the other has a long straight sword, in the Ghent version one has a spear and one a rod. The body painting of snakes and a human mask on the chest is less emphasized on the London than on the Ghent figures, where the 'Mannerist' style more appropriate to the White drawings of a decade later is used, with animal masks on shoulder and knee. These de Heere Britons have usually been thought to reflect the influence of American Indian depictions (as with White), but in fact there seems no reason to look for any such connection. Body paint, long shields, swords and spears are all to be found in the classical texts relating to the Celts, while the rather melancholy shaggy heads come very close to de Heere's drawings of the 'Wilde Irish' in both his MSS, themselves not drawn from life but from an earlier drawing now lost but represented by a surviving woodcut of *c.* 1540–50.[35] His ancient Britons then are consciously composed artifacts but need owe nothing to America.

The drawings of Britons by John White and those engraved by De Bry in 1590, and copied by John Speed in 1611, are another and more complicated story. Kendrick first drew attention to these in 1950, and the White and De Bry versions have recently been published with comment by Paul Hulton, who deals with the complex relationship of these with the drawings of Jacques Le Moyne of which mention has just been made.[36] The investigation can, however, be taken yet a stage further. White's drawings are in the main of the South-Eastern Algonquian Indians, and the local fauna and flora, encountered by him as artist to the 1585 Virginia expedition. To these he added the two 1577 Frobisher Eskimos, five drawings of ancient Britons, and five Turkish and oriental figures: none of these have titles but suggest collection for a costume book of the type made by de Heere a decade earlier. In 1590 Theodor De Bry, a native of Liège and as a Protestant refugee set up as a printer and engraver in Frankfort-am-Main, published the first part of his magnificent *America*, with the text of Thomas Harriot's *A briefe and true report of the new found land of Virginia*, and engravings from White's drawings. There then follows, with a separate title-page

SOM PICTURE OF THE PICTES WHICH IN THE OLDE tyme dyd habite one part of the great Bretainne. THE PAINTER OF WHOM I HAVE had the first of the Inhabitans of Virginia, give my allso thees 5. Figures fallowinge, fownd as hy did assured my in a oolld English cronicle, the which I wold well sett to the ende of thees first Figures, for to showe how that the Inhabitants of the great Bretannie have bin in times past as sauuage as those of Virginia.

Poor De Bry! His English is a bit fractured, but he was producing simultaneously Latin, English, French and German versions of his book, a remarkable feat of publication in 1590 (or at any time), and he firmly made the ethnographical comparison which was to influence all subsequent antiquaries. But Hulton has pointed out that De Bry has confused his sources, for the 'Pictish' drawings are not by White, but Jacques Le Moyne, though so close as to imply that both artists had copied from a common source, which must be De Bry's 'oolld English cronicle'. We can, in agreeing with Hulton, go further and be more precise about this lost source.

In the first place it is clear that the old chronicle, whatever its real nature may have been, was not English but Scottish. Its concentration on Picts – three figures as against two 'neighbours unto the Picts' – makes this point, as do, as we shall see, the careful archaeological details in the drawings. A further point is the short curved sword anachronistically carried by all but one figure in De Bry as in White's

SOM PICTVRE,
OF THE PICTES
WHICH IN THE OLDE
tyme dyd habite one part of the
great Bretainne.

*THE PAINTER OF WHOM J HAVE
had the firſt of the Inhabitans of Virginia, giue my allſo thees 5. Figures
fallowinge, fownd as hy did aſſured my in a oolld Engliſh cronicle, the which
I woldwell ſett to the cnde of thees firſt Figures, for to showe how that
the Inhabitants of the great Bretannie haue bin in ti-
mes paſt as ſauuage as thoſe of
Virginia.*

E

2 Theodor De Bry's third title-page to his America (1590), giving the alleged
source of the drawings and a direct comparison between ancient Britons and
American Indians.

3 De Bry's engraving IIII from America (1590), of 'a man of nation neighbour into the Picte', with globular spear-butt (from Dio Cassius) and anachronistic falchion.

4 De Bry's engraving V, of a 'women nighbour to the Pictes', with spear
and falchion as in the companion male figure.

5 Ancient British woman, woodcut from John Speed, Historie of Great
Britaine *(1611), copied from De Bry's engraving V (see fig. 4 above) but
more decorously dressed and with body painting and a hare added.*

6 *Ancient British man, woodcut from John Speed's* Historie *(1611); a free version of De Bry's engraving I of a Pict, and close to John White's drawing of 1588 (see plate 17).*

drawings, one of which however carries a sword of fifteenth–sixteenth-century English type. The curved sword had been taken by the present writer to be 'a sort of fantastic semi-oriental scimitar'[37] and indeed De Bry called it 'a cimeterre or turkie sword'. The type appears at first sight to be (if again anachronistically) paralleled by the short sword with curved blade and a bird-headed hilt of early seventeenth-century date which there is reason to believe was known as a 'Scots fauchion' or 'Scottish hanger' and regarded as 'auncient' in the later seventeenth century.[38] Unfortunately the resemblance is not close enough to confirm the Scottish origin of De Bry's old chronicle, used by both White and Le Moyne, and put the falchion type back into the sixteenth century.

When we turn to the archaeological details derived from the classical texts, the 'chronicle' and its illustrations were explicit, and used or quoted verbatim in a form transmitted to De Bry's text two crucial authorities, both from the Greek; Herodian (fl.AD 235) and Dio Cassius (AD 160–230) on the Severan campaigns against the Caledonii and Maeatae of North Britain in AD 208–209. Both texts were available to scholars, including Camden, who printed them in full, but did not assign them to the Picts, but to Britons in general, mentioning elsewhere 'those ancient and barbarous Britons, that afterwards, went by the name of Picti'. The De Bry source must have specifically assigned the passages to the Picts. That it must have been written as well as pictorial, is shown by the references to iron torcs (found only in Herodian): in De Bry's words 'they carried abowt their necks one ayerne ring, and another abowt the middle of their bodye, abowt the bellye', and he refers to a sword chain, in this case from Diodorus Siculus. He and others, including Dio Cassius, have the narrow oval shield, twisted torcs, nakedness, head-hunting and body painting, especially Herodian – 'They paint their bodies with sundry colours, with all kinds of animals represented in them'. Finally, only in Dio do we have a reference to 'a short spear with a bronze apple on the end of the shaft, so that when it is shaken it clashes', taken up by De Bry as a spear 'which hath at the lowe end a rownde bowlle', and like the torcs appears prominently in the drawings. Here direct archaeological confirmation is provided, for such globular bronze spear-butts are a peculiarly Scottish type represented by examples or casting-moulds from eight sites from East Lothian to Orkney.[39] After De Bry globular spear-butts became popular with any or all Ancient Britons, as for instance in John Speed's *Historie* of 1611, and the portrait of 'A Britaine' on the title-page of his *Theatre of the Empire of Great*

7 *Detail of engraved title-page of John Speed's* Theatre of the Empire of Great Britaine *(1611), showing 'A Britaine', a noble figure ultimately from De Bry: also shown (not illustrated here) are a Roman, a Saxon, a Dane and a Norman.*

8 Boadicea, Queen of the Iceni, reviewing her troops and looking very
like Queen Elizabeth 1 of England (except for the sacred hare); *woodcut
from Raphael Holinshed's* Chronicles *of 1578*.

Britaine of the same year. In all, the De Bry engravings, and his short but accurate text, completely altered the view of the ancient Briton, visually and conceptually, after 1590. Bryony Orme nicely made the point that Holinshed's picture of Boadicea (1577) shows the Queen of the Iceni crowned and robed, indistinguishable from Elizabeth Queen of England (except for a large divinatory hare under her arm), whereas Speed's 1611 portrait is an improved version of De Bry's 'Women nighbour to the Pictes'.[40]

The American impact on Europe was widespread and touched on every aspect of thought and literature: Montaigne's famous essays are so well known as to need no comment and they were early available in English with John Florio's translation of 1603. It was inevitable that ancient Britons were compared with modern American Indians, and Samuel Daniel made an interesting comparison, in the *First Part of the Historie of England* (1612), when he wrote of the country and its earliest inhabitants as having been 'a multitude of pettie regiments' as in the 'west world lately discovered'.[41] This, of course, was echoed by Aubrey when he wrote, 'I believe that there were several *Reguli* which often made war upon another', though he did not immediately draw a parallel between ancient Wiltshire and the New World. In the meantime Robert Burton (who read everything) had in 1621 recommended as a cure for melancholy the pleasure of reading of 'those parts of America, set out, and curiously cut in pictures, in *Fratres à Bry*' and elsewhere exclaims, 'See but what *Cesar* reports of us, and *Tacitus* of those Germans, they were once as uncivil as they in *Virginia*'.[42] Nathanael Carpenter in 1625 said the same: the first people of Germany and Britain lived on roots and herbs and were 'little different from the present Americans'.[43] By the mid century the comparison was becoming a commonplace, and when Thomas Hobbes in 1651 made his famous estimate of the life of primitive man being nasty, brutish and short, he goes on: 'the savage people in many places of America ... live at this day in that brutish manner, as I said before'.[44] Aubrey wrote his unpublished comment about 1659, and in 1691 the naturalist John Ray, in his *Wisdom of God in his Creation* felt that any civilized country was to be preferred to 'a rude and unpolished America peopled with slothful and naked Indians, instead of well-built Houses, living in pitiful Huts and Cabans, made of poles set end-ways'. Even if some of the original encounters with the American Indians, from the first voyage of Columbus to Arthur Barlow in 1584 finding them 'such as lived after the golden age', encouraged a favourable view of 'soft primitivism', for the early antiquaries they, on the whole, ranked at the bottom of the scale of civility, and with them went their counterparts, the ancient Britons.

In the next chapter we shall turn to the conceptual problems presented by prehistoric tools and weapons of stone or bronze, but we may conclude our estimate of the American influence by noting how ethnographical parallels helped in establishing the status of stone tools in Britain. Although Sir William Dugdale in 1656 had identified stone axes found in Warwickshire as 'weapons used by the Britons before the art of making arms of brass or iron was known',[45] it seems to have been Dr Plot in 1686 who first published the comment 'which how they may be fastened to a *helve*, may be seen in the *Musaeum Ashmoleanum* where are several *Indian* ones of the like kind, fitted up in the same order as when formerly used.'[46] Edward Lhuyd, Plot's assistant keeper in the Ashmolean and evidently influenced by the same specimens, wrote to his friend Richard Richardson in 1699 of flint arrow-heads 'they are just the same chip'd flints the natives of New England head their arrows with at this day, and there also several stone hatchets found in this kingdom, not unlike those of the Americans.'[47] Lhuyd was opposing the belief current in Scotland in his day that flint arrow-heads were 'elf-bolts' shot by fairies, and three-quarters of a century later the same situation was faced and countered by no less a person than Dr Samuel Johnson.

In 1775 Johnson made his famous journey to the Western Isles, no doubt fresh from reading his friend John Hawkesworth's journalistic write-up of the first voyage of Captain James Cook and Joseph Banks, and seeing one of Banks's exhibitions.[48] On the island of Raasay he wrote of its early inhabitants

A proof much stronger of the distance at which the first possessors of this island lived from the present time, is afforded by the stone heads of arrows which are very frequently picked up. The people call them *Elf-bolts*, and believe the fairies shoot them at the cattle. They nearly resemble those which Mr *Banks* has lately brought from the savage countries in the Pacific Ocean, and must have been made by a nation to which the use of metals was unknown.[49]

Though the scene has shifted from America to the South Pacific, Johnson's acute observation and sound common sense unwittingly led him to the same conclusions as Lhuyd.

4

Time, technology and the monuments

The antiquaries of the late sixteenth and early seventeenth centuries
were faced with the problem of assessing the cultural status of the
ancient Briton and equally facing something of a dilemma inherent in
their textual sources and their new knowledge of the Americas. The
Biblical story was one of degeneracy as one moved westward from the
civilized ancient orient with only very basic skills of survival and
existence preserved, and this seemed confirmed by the discovery in the
furthest west of stone-using, non-agricultural, hunting and food-
gathering Indians, whose technology, as we saw in the last chapter,
could provide a convincing parallel to that suggested by actual finds of
stone implements attributable to the earliest inhabitants of Britain.

In the absence of an historical sense of internal chronology and
development, immediately pre-Roman could be indistinguishable
from immediately post-Diluvial, even though on accepted time scales
nearly two millennia intervened. The idea of internal social and
technological development, of progress itself within a society was
difficult to grasp, and as the earliest recorded history of England
presented itself as a series of invasions and conquests – Romans,
Saxons, Danes, Normans – an 'Invasion Hypothesis' was the inevitable
model for antecedent times, and indeed remained so for archaeologists
until recent times.[1] In such a context Caesar's reference to an
immigration into south-east England 'from Belgium' was eagerly taken
up and much was made of his distinction between this region – the
'maritime districts' – and the 'people of the interior'. 'The interior of
Britain', he wrote, 'is inhabited by a people who, according to oral
tradition – so the Britons themselves say – are aboriginal . . . the people
of the interior do not, for the most part, cultivate grain, but live on milk
and meat and clothe themselves with skins' (Caesar, *BG* V. 12, 14).
Strabo, enlarging on this in Book IV of his *Geography*, had written,

'some of them have not the art to make cheese, though they have much milk; others of them know neither the art of horticulture, nor any other kind of husbandry.' This, in a seventeenth-century England deservedly proud of its dairy products, provoked the sarcasm of Sir Thomas Browne in his *Vulgar Errors* of 1646, quoting

Strabo, who to the dishonour of our *Predecessors* and the disparagement of those who glory in the antiquity of their *Ancestors*, affirms the *Britains* were so simple, that though they abounded in Milk, they had not the artifice of Cheese.

These aboriginal Britons were clearly the first colonists of the island after the Flood, and as such could justly be compared, as non-agricultural, skin-clad, hunters and pastoralists, with the American Indians, and like them could have had stone tools and weapons, waiting to be identified and classified in a modern Baconian manner.

We shall turn to this approach, so fundamental to the emergence of what was to become archaeology out of antiquarianism, but a brief consideration of the knowledge and availability of the crucial and influential classical texts from the sixteenth century is not without intrest. Camden gave, in his section of the *Britannia*, 'The Manners of the BRITAINS', the relevant passages from Caesar, Strabo, Diodorus Siculus, Pomponius Mela, Tacitus, Dio Cassius and Herodian: that from Caesar is abbreviated and conflated. With the Italian Renaissance printed texts had become early available: Caesar's *Commentaries* on the Gallic War (*De Bello Gallico*) was first printed in 1511 in Venice, Tacitus in Rome four years later. In England, as early as 1530, there appeared Caesar's *Commentaryes newly translated owte of latin into Englysshe as much as concerneth thys realm of England* and attributed to John Tiptoft, Earl of Worcester. Now he, a singularly brutal Yorkist, was executed in 1470, but had in early life enjoyed the reputation of a distinguished Latinist after study in Italy. If the translation is by him, it must have been from a manuscript presumably acquired by him on his travels, but even in 1530 it was a remarkably early contribution to antiquarian scholarship in the vernacular. By 1604 Sir Clement Edmondes had printed his translation and *Observations upon Caesar's Commentaries*; Sir Henry Savile translated *Fower Bookes of the Histories ... and the Life of Agricola* by Tacitus in 1591, Richard Greneway the *Annals* and the *Germania* in 1598. By 1610 and Philemon Holland's translation of Camden, the texts were easily available even to the reader who had no Latin, and were proportionately influential.

Britons and stone tools

When we come to the recognition of stone tools attributable to the ancient Britons, touched on in the last chapter in the context of ethnographical comparisons with the New World, we find a by no means simple story. They had in the first place to be distinguished from the other forms of stones which came to be collected and classified from the sixteenth century onwards – minerals and crystals, gems and ores, earths and what were to be grouped as 'fossils' in the modern restricted sense, separate from everything else which was 'dug up'. Ulisse Aldrovandi in the sixteenth-century University of Bologna was Professor *de fossilibus*, which meant all metals and stones extracted from the earth. The Renaissance naturalists' difficulties in recognizing fossils as representing extinct organisms are well known and have been much discussed;[2] in England their true nature was recognized by Robert Hooke and Christopher Merret independently in 1665–6, but acceptance was not universal among even the best naturalists of the day, such as Martin Lister the great conchologist; Edward Lhuyd and John Ray were very uncertain. Stone tools presented in part the same difficulties as fossils in that they had to be distinguished from other 'Formed Stones' with well defined shapes such as crystals, with which, among 'Regular Stones', flint arrowheads were classified by the botanist Nehemiah Grew in his 1681 catalogue of the museum of the Royal Society as among the works of nature, and Martin Lister held the same view. As with fossils the issue could be clouded by the metaphysical presuppositions of the revived Neoplatonism of the time: if every physical object represented the expression of an antecedent Platonic Ideal of itself present in the mind of God, it was impossible to be sure of its origin as a mundane phenomenon, for a fossil could have been a living organism or the realization in inert stone of the same Ideal. A barbed and tanged flint arrowhead looked like a humanly made projectile point, but if man might flake it, God could make it equally convincingly as a work of his natural creation.

The first recognition of prehistoric stone tools as such took place in sixteenth-century Italy. Here there had been formed the earliest collections of natural and artificial objects, as Cabinets of Rarities or Curiosities, often in parallel with gardens of plants and medicinal herbs, and such collections of objects for study by natural philosophers rather than art galleries for the connoisseur might contain not only ethnographical material, but local antiquities including objects such as flint arrowheads. In arranging and cataloguing these museums a decision had to be made as to their status, regularly formed stones or ancient artifacts, and here the ethnographical specimens would by analogy favour the latter explanation. Priority in this crucial recognition is usually assigned to Michele Mercati (1541–93), superintendent of the botanic gardens in the Vatican, but the catalogue of his collections of stones, minerals and fossils made in 1572–81 remained unpublished until 1717 and so had no influence on foreign scholars at the time. But at Bologna there were notable contemporary museums, such as those of Antonio Giganti (1535–98) and above all Ulisse Aldrovandi (1522–1605). Both had New World stone tools and bows and arrows, and Aldrovandi local flint arrowheads which he recognized as such and attributed them to the ancient Romans (fair enough in an Italy with no concept of a prehistoric past). His catalogue, published posthumously in 1648, *Musaeum Metallicum in Libros IIII distributum . . .* was to be quoted in Britain by Sir Robert Sibbald in 1684 and Dr Plot in 1686, and must have been the main vehicle of transmission of the Italian identification to British antiquaries.[3]

In Denmark the distinguished antiquary Ole Worm not only wrote his influential book on Danish antiquities, *Danicorum Monumentorum Libri Sex* of 1643, but formed a famous museum in Copenhagen containing prehistoric objects as well as fossils, plants, birds, animals, and ethnographical specimens. In his catalogue of this published in the year after his death, in 1655, he was uncertain about his local flint arrowheads and daggers – *de quibus dubito Artisne aut Natura sint opera* – but one at least he thought *potius Arte quam Natura elaboratum esse*, yet he could regard a shaft-hole stone axe as the fossil of an original in iron.[4]

In Britain, while, as we saw in the last chapter, Dugdale had recognized the true nature of flint axe-heads as early as 1656, the first reasoned statement on prehistoric stone tools was that of Dr Plot in his *Natural History of Staffordshire* of 1686. He starts with a reference to Caesar which we saw becoming a commonplace

Caesar acquaints us that the *Britans* had *Iron*, yet they finding it then by the *sea* side only . . . we have reason to believe that for the most part at lest they sharpen'd their *warlike instruments* rather with *stones* than *metall*, especiall in the more *Northerly* and *inland Countries*, where they sometimes meet with *flints* in the shape of *arrowheads*.

Plot illustrates a Staffordshire find of a large barbed and tanged arrowhead and quotes Scottish finds to which we shall shortly turn, and goes on, 'Nor did the *Britans* only head their *arrows* with *flint*, but

9 Staffordshire antiquities drawn and engraved by Michael Burghers for Plot's Natural History of Stafford-shire (1686). 1, *flint arrowhead*; 2, *flint knife*; 3, *stone axe*; 5–8 *bronze axes, chisel and spearhead*. Nos 9–11 are the late Anglo-Saxon cross-shafts at Checkley.

also their *matarae* or *British darts*, which were thrown by those that fought in *Essedis*', illustrating what would now be classed as a plano-convex knife with serrated edges and ignoring the technological improbability of stone-using savages constructing war-chariots. 'We may conclude', he writes, 'not only that these *arrow* and *Spear-heads*, are all artificial, whatever is pretended, but also that they had anciently some way of working of *flints* by the *toole*, which may be seen by the marks.' Sir Robert Sibbald, Plot continues, thought the Britons had been taught this art by the Romans, and quotes Aldrovandi's *Museum metallicum*. 'However still it not being hence deducible, but they may be *British*, they are not ill placed here, whatever original they have had from either *Nation*. Either the *Britans*, *Romans*, or *both*, also made them *Axes* of Stone', and illustrating one, he goes on to make the ethnographical comparison of its hafting we have already quoted.

Plot made reference to Sir Robert Sibbald (1641–1722), the Scottish antiquary, who in 1684 had published his Latin *Scotia Illustrata sive Prodromus Historiae Naturalis* in Edinburgh.[5] This takes us into a very odd world, where the interpretation of prehistoric flint arrowheads, and stone axes, was bedevilled by the persistent fantasies of international and insular folklore, as Lhuyd and Johnson were independently to find. Lhuyd noted when Sibbald's guest in 1699, in Scotland 'the most Curious as well the Vulgar' – obviously including his host here – believed that flint arrowheads fell from the sky as 'Elf Bolts', used and made by witches and fairies. 'For my part', wrote Lhuyd to a friend, 'I must crave leave to suspend my faith, until I see one of them descend.'[6] But Sir Robert had no doubts. In the *Prodromus*, he gives a catalogue of natural and artificial 'figured stones', and by far the longest entry is given to *Lapides, quos nostratibus Sagittae Lamiarum dicuntur*, quoting at length from Gordon of Straloch's unpublished *Aberdoniae utriusque Descriptio*, which describes barbed flint arrow-heads in detail and declares them to appear from nowhere in fields and public ways and to be known in the local vernacular as 'Elf-Arrowheads', adding *Faunos enim Lamiasque et id genus Spiritum Elfs vocant*. But *lamia* is good classical Latin for a sinister witch, and Scottish witches shot elf-bolts at cattle and persons. In her extraordinary 'confession' made at her trial for witchcraft in 1662 Isobel Gowdie admitted she had not only flicked a flint arrowhead with her finger and thumb at a gentleman (she fortunately missed) but, recounting her visit to fairyland under the Downie Hills said, 'As for Elf-arrow-heids, the Divel shapes them with his awin hand . . . Elf-boyes, who whyttis and dightis them with a sharp thing lyke a paking neidle'.[7] The Reverend Robert Kirk, a learned friend of both Sibbald and Robert Boyle, wrote in 1691 a strangely detached, almost anthropological, account of *The Secret Common-wealth of Elves and Fairies*[8] in which he implicitly believed, recounting how his parishioners 'sene or hallow themselves, their corns and cattell, from the shots and stealth of these wandring Tribes ... to save them from the Arrows that fly in the Dark', reported to Boyle, 'I have had barbed Arrow-heads of yellow flint, that could not be cut so small and neat, of so brittle a Substance, by all the Airt of Man.' In the catalogue of Sibbald's museum of 1697,[9] under 'Regular Stones' appears 'Anchorites; the flat Bolthead' and the stories of elves and fairies repeated. In the *Prodromus* another legend going back at least to Pliny is perpetuated, that of stone axes, especially those perforated with a shaft-hole, as thunder bolts descending from the heavens with lightning: Sibbald describes two stone shaft-hole axes under *Ceraunia Lapis a figura Fulminis nomen habet*, and quotes Aldrovandi. In the catalogue of the museum of Lodovico Moscardo of 1672, quoted by Plot, two polished axe-heads are depicted as 'Saette o Fulmini'. In the world of Scottish antiquarianism the supernatural died hard, and 'elf-bolts' could be talked of, if half facetiously, up to recent years.

By the opening years of the eighteenth century the situation had settled down, and stone implements were generally accepted as prehistoric artifacts. The current views were set out, surprisingly enough, by the Oxford antiquary Thomas Hearne,[10] normally devoted only to manuscript sources. In 1707 he recorded in his notebook the collections of Dr Arthur Charlett, Master of University College

Above stairs Dr Charlett has Roman Urns &c. Abt. fourteen years since on ye North-West of London was found large Elephant Bones, amongst ym Teeth, & near to them a flint like our Scotch Elf Arrows, which some Curious Persons are apt to think was yt with wch ye Elephant was kill'd. Dr Charlett has it.

Hearne later published this find in his *Collectanea* I (1715) and by a freak of chance it survives, and is in the British Museum. It is a fine and massive hand-axe of the Middle Palaeolithic, 18 cm long, and only Hearne could have compared it with the delicate little Scottish arrow-heads. The elephant's bones could have been those of a mammoth.

Hearne was still interested in flints in the next year, when he wrote on 22 November 1708 to Francis Brokesby

I am intirely of Sir William Dugdale's opinion that the Flints he tells us to be found at Oldbury are British Axes. There have been of them found at other places, & other

Instruments of Flint, as their Arrow and Spear Heads, sufficiently show that they made use of Flint, the way of working in Iron being quite unknown to them.

The Romans, he goes on, used flint for weapons too, and could have taught the Britons 'yet for all that I am inclin'd to think that most if not all these found in this Isle are British . . . I have seen of their Arrow Heads my self, we having several of them in our Repositories' and they are found in the north of England, 'but more commonly in Scotland, especially near Aberdeene, where they are called Elf-Arrows & they think they drop from the Clouds.' Stone axes would be hafted 'in the same manner as the Indians use at this day, who have likewise Flint-Axes, several of which are lodg'd in Mr Ashmole's museum.' Two of Dugdale's axes from the Oldbury (Warwickshire) hoard were in Oxford at the time, one in the Ashmolean and the other in the collection of John Pointer of Merton.[11] Hearne would have seen Sibbald's *Prodromus* and may well have talked with Lhuyd.

By the last decades of the seventeenth century, then, the British antiquaries were prepared to regard flint and stone implements not as naturally formed Regular Stones, but as the artifacts of the ancient Britons. By many historians of archaeology this has been hailed as the first recognition of a technological Stone Age, chronologically antecedent to the use of metal for edge-tools, and as such anticipating the Three Ages system of the Danish archaeologists of the 1830s. In fact the evidence of the contemporary antiquaries suggests that this concept of a long temporal succession was still quite foreign to their minds, and for them the recognition of stone tools served rather to reinforce the barbarity of the Britons 'of the interior' as compared with those using bronze, iron and gold in the 'maritime districts' in Caesar's time. It must have been Aldrovandi's attribution of flint arrowheads to the primeval Romans that led Sibbald and others to think, in the prevailing innocence of anachronism, that these ancient Italians would be indistinguishable from the Romans who entered Britain under Caesar and Claudius, skilled flint workers who could have taught their craft to the British savages. Even if the Britons had somehow achieved this technology themselves (like the American Indians), this need not have been at a period necessarily very remote from Caesar. The stereotype of a brutish stone-using ancient British hunter was in fact to inhibit the understanding of the actual antiquities of prehistoric Britain up to the nineteenth century, and a further conceptual difficulty had to be surmounted, that of a technological stage in which copper and bronze edge-tools followed those of stone and preceded those of iron.

The problem of bronze

The writer has recently discussed this problem of the acceptance of prehistoric bronze implements by the early antiquaries, and here it is sufficient to review the evidence in its wider context of the evolution of the concept of the cultural status of the ancient Briton.[12] We may start parenthetically with a note on terminology. Today, the alloy 'bronze' is distinguished as that of copper and tin from 'brass', that of copper and zinc, but this is a usage dating only from the last century, as the *OED*, beginning publication in 1884, states that 'bronze' in this sense 'has recently been adopted'. 'Brass' and 'brazen' for both alloys of copper goes back to an Old English *braes*, without cognates in other European languages, which use versions of an originally Italian *bronzo*, and its adoption in nineteenth-century English seems an archaeological as much as a lexical innovation, prompted by the Bronze Age of the Danish archaeologists of the 1830s, popularized in translation from 1848 and given currency by Daniel Wilson in his *Archaeology and Prehistoric Annals of Scotland* (1851) and Sir John Lubbock in his *Prehistoric Times* of 1865: Wilson incidentally 'coined the word *prehistoric* for my own use'. In all the earlier antiquarian literature therefore 'brass' is our 'bronze' (in Britain the copper–zinc alloy is not earlier than Roman).

It is now convenient to return to Robert Plot in 1686, whose opinions on flint and stone tools have just been quoted at length. Having dealt with these British antiquities in Staffordshire, he goes on to Roman roads, mosaic pavements, what he thought might be Roman barrows, and 'their *instruments* of Warr', beginning with 'a brass head of the *bolt* of a *Catapulta*' and three others, one of which he illustrates: it is a bronze age palstave. A flat bronze axe, 'I take to have been the head of a Roman *Securis*', a late bronze age socketed chisel 'the head of a Roman *rest*, used to support the *lituus*' and a socketed spear-head a '*Roman Venabulum* or hunting spear.' The question of their being perhaps pre-Roman is not entertained. This view was to be held by Hearne at the beginning of the next century, and in Scotland by Sibbald, where Alexander Gordon would support the Roman origin of prehistoric bronzes as late as 1726. But before that the problem was to receive the attention of a first-class mind, that of Edward Lhuyd, who succeeded Plot as Keeper of the Ashmolean Museum in 1691.

In 1692–3 the young and brilliant Edmund Gibson put out his first printed Proposals for a new English-language edition of Camden's *Britannia*, brought up to date by contributions from contemporary scholars. He was able to assemble a remarkable group of historians and antiquaries, not least Lhuyd, to translate, revise and augment the entries for Wales. The revised Camden with Lhuyd's additions came out in 1695, and he was in the meantime planning his *Archaeologia Britannica* in four volumes, the third of which was to be 'An Account of all such Monuments now remaining in *Wales* as are presumed to be *British*; and either older, or not much later than the *Roman* conquest: *viz* their Camps and Burial Places; their monuments called *Cromlecheu* and *Meinieugwyr*; their Coyns, Arms, Amulets &c.' This was announced in 1697, but Lhuyd unexpectedly died in 1709 with only the first projected volume, the work on comparative Celtic philology, published in 1707. His *Britannia* entries however give us an indication of his thinking on bronze implements.[13]

His starting point was a prescient observation by Camden himself, discussing what we now see as a Late Bronze Age hoard from near St Michael's Mount in Cornwall, first recorded in Leland. Camden describes the hoard as of 'spear-heads, axes and swords, all wrapp'd up in Linnen, of the same sort with those found long ago in *Hircinia* in Germany, and others lately in Wales. For it is plain from the Monuments of Antiquity, that the Greeks, Cimbrians and Britons, made use of brass-weapons'. 'Our author', says Lhuyd, 'supposes them British' and so comparable with what he is describing from Wales, which must have been a Middle Bronze Age hoard, largely of rapiers, from Beddgelert and another hoard from Deganwy, with palstaves like one from Moel y Henllys in Montgomeryshire. Going back to St Michael's Mount and Camden's verdict of ancient British bronzes he goes on, 'and indeed it is not to be doubted that they were so, if the brass Arms he mentions were really swords of that metal. For my part I must confess, that for a long time I suspected these instruments Roman, supposing them to be too artificial to have been made by the Britains before the Romans civiliz'd them.' Taking into account a Late Bronze Age gold torc from Harlech which he also argues is British, and the fact of a British gold coinage, 'I know not but they might have more arts than we commonly allow them, and therefore must suspend my judgement.' In 1701 he wrote to a correspondent about 'some of those copper or brass axes' being not only English or Welsh but they 'are also found in the bogs of Ireland, so that probably they are not Roman, but British'. Lhuyd's carefully considered change of view to favour a British rather than a Roman origin for the bronzes shows exactly what an inhibiting effect the stereotype of the barbarous Briton could have on the understanding of a developmental sequence.

In Oxford in 1709, the year of Lhuyd's death, a rearguard action on ancient bronzes was mounted by (not surprisingly) Thomas Hearne, who continued his short, but as it turned out unfortunate interest in prehistoric matters begun the year before, by entering into a discussion on prehistoric bronze tools, based wholly on misunderstood or irrelevant literary sources.[14] It began by Ralph Thoresby, the Leeds wool merchant and antiquary, reporting the discovery of a hoard of Late Bronze Age socketed axes at Osmondthick in West Yorkshire: 'some suppose them to have been *Arrows heads*, or *Axes* of the ancient *Britains*, others of the Roman *Catapultae*', but Thoresby opts for the 'heads of spears or walking staves of the civilized *Britains*', though unlike those 'described by *Speed* in their Portraitures, taken I presume from ancient MSS' – a wise comment on the figures deriving from De Bry discussed in the last chapter. Hearne would have none of this, and replied at great length (22 pages of closely printed text) demonstrating the axes to be Roman. The Britons had stone tools and so did the Romans (this of course from Aldrovandi) and the Britons probably came from Gaul, but the axes do not fit the description of any Gaulish weapon mentioned in the classical texts and so cannot be Gaulish or British. Nor can they be Saxon, as Verstegen does not show such weapons in his illustration of Hengist and Horsa (a wholly fanciful picture showing the Saxons armed with crossbows), nor Danish as nothing like them appears in the pages of Ole Worm. 'These *Instruments* are *Roman Chissels*, which were used to cut and polish the *Stones* in their *Tents*' and also for road building and in 'making their Aggeres'. Dr Richard Richardson, Thoresby's friend, contributed a welcome note of sense in a letter (also printed by Hearne) saying the bronzes were axes, mounted in the manner accepted today on an angled or knee-haft. Hearne of course was doing no more than putting up the case for the Ancients, with their appeal to revered texts, rather than that of the empirical Moderns represented by Richardson.

Hearne also published another find reported by Thoresby, an Early Bronze Age cremation in an inverted cinerary urn with a bronze razor, a shaft-hole stone axe and a perforated hone, from Broughton in Craven. Thoresby took the finds to be Roman, but Hearne added his comments – 'I believe they are much more *modern* . . . I do not take these to be *Roman* but *Danish antiquities*, and owing to them at such time as they had settled themselves in *these parts* . . . 'Tis well known the *Danes* us'd *Urns*.' This view was based on Late Bronze Age cinerary urns described by Ole Worm, with the assumption that as they were found in modern Denmark they were the products of the historical

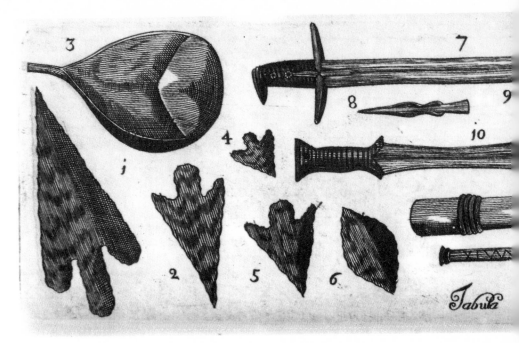

10 Scottish antiquities including flint arrowheads (1–6), and Bronze Age spears and sword (8–10) engraved by Robert Miln for Sibbald's Miscellanea . . . (1710). No.7, believed by Sibbald to be a great iron Caledonian sword as described by Tacitus, is a weapon not earlier than the late sixteenth century, probably Polish.

Danes who had occupied England in the ninth and tenth centuries AD, a fatal misunderstanding which we shall see also misled other antiquaries with other antiquities.

In Scotland the Romans held the field. Sir Robert Sibbald in his *Miscellanea quaedam eruditae antiquitatis* (1710) and Alexander Gordon in his *Itinerarium Septentrionalis* (1726) illustrated and described between them some twenty or so Early to Late Bronze Age objects, Sibbald including those from an important Late Bronze Age hoard from Orrock in Fife; Gordon's bronzes were mainly in the collection of his patron, Sir John Clerk of Penicuik (1676–1755). Both assigned them to the Romans; though Gordon thought of Early Bronze Age axes, 'it is disputable whether these are *Roman* or not' in the end he (no doubt expressing Sir John's views) classed them all as Roman: '*Hastae* or *Roman Spears*', and swords '*Roman* I make no doubt', while a spear-butt is a '*Roman Tuba* or Trumpet'. In England a Late Bronze Age situla found near Chester about 1718 was described as 'a Roman Camp Kettle', but in Wales the Reverend Henry Rowlands, an

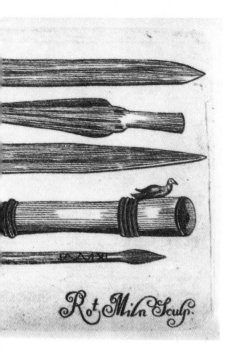
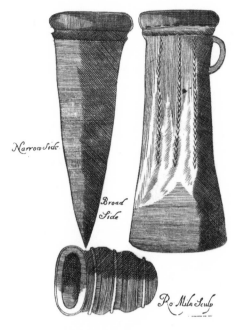

11 *Socketed bronze axe and Bronze Age pot from Aberdeenshire, engraved by Robert Miln for Sibbald's* Miscellanea . . . (1710).

Anglesey vicar who was a friend of Lhuyd, illustrated part of a hoard of Late Bronze socketed axes from his own weird drawings as 'a Parcel of *British* weapons' in his *Mona Antiqua Restaurata* (1723 but circulating in MS by about 1710). By mid-century the acceptance of prehistoric bronzes seems to have been general, and was summed up by William Borlase in his *Antiquities . . . of the County of Cornwall* (1754). Discussing a hoard of late bronze age socketed axes from Carn Brea, and quoting Camden on the St Michael's Mount find, he decides that in arms, if not tools, there must have been a development in antiquity. 'The most ancient weapons were neither armed with Brass nor Iron . . . the Britons . . . had flint heads for their spears and arrows, if they had not also hatchets of the same substance.' Copper was then used, and soon its alloys, and 'with Metal it was found much easier to head their spears and Arrows, then to grind a stone into the necessary offensive form.' Iron was used by the Britons late and rarely: copper working he hints might have been introduced from outside as it was known 'very early among the Orientals'.

By the eighteenth century the antiquaries had stumbled, individually and indirectly, towards some sort of an appreciation of stone-using communities among the ancient British population, and even, with Borlase, thinking of these as vaguely chronologically earlier than the metal-using Britons of Caesar. For most, though, the distinction between Britons of the Interior and those of the Maritime Districts seemed to explain technological disparities without the need of any awkward developmental process and a time scale, and as for bronzes, they remained difficult. In the Americas (and later in the South Seas) what amounted to stone age communities were observed and made use of as ethnographical comparisons; in Black Africa flourishing iron age chiefdoms might offer instructive examples of a final metallurgical stage, but no traveller had encountered a Bronze Age. Caesar's remarks that 'tin is found in the country in the inland and iron in the maritime districts, but the latter only in small quantities; bronze is imported' were eagerly taken up, and in particular the final phrase, which would dispose of an indigenous stone–bronze–iron technological sequence in favour of a sophisticated introduction by peoples of a higher culture in search of the tin necessary for the copper alloy, known as Borlase said 'very early among the Orientals'.

Optimism and Phoenicians

These Orientals were to confuse British antiquarianism for centuries. In the search for respectable ancestors among the ancient Britons, and for an optimistic rather than a wholly pessimistic picture of the status of the earliest colonists after the Flood, the Phoenicians first made their baleful appearance on a British stage in the sixteenth century. In his *De rebus Albionicus* of 1590, John Twyne, seeking an alternative to the legend of the Trojan Brutus, produced instead those great navigators of antiquity the Phoenicians, making their last western landfall in Britain. The idea does not seem to have been particularly noticed, but in 1646 the French scholar Samuel Bochart (1599–1667) published his popular and very influential *Geographia Sacra*, which brought the Phoenicians to be the founding fathers of ancient Europe. This was taken up with enthusiasm and prolixity by Aylett Sammes ('the most unaccountable and ridulous Plagiary and Buffon that ever had his name upon the title page of any book what so ever' as Bishop Nicolson exploded)[15] in his *Britannia Antiqua Illustrata* of 1676, where as we saw he repudiated an English Channel land-bridge and discoursed on ancient British chariotry. His account of the post-Diluvial colonization of Britain was complex and at least original. The descendants of Gomer were to be found in the Cimmerioi of the Pontic Steppe, who were in turn the historical Cimbri of northern Europe,[16] who coming to Britain brought a Teutonic language, and there they are on Sammes's map trekking their way with a covered wagon and in tall hats from the Black Sea to Kent. But these were only the aborigines, for 'The first discovery of this ISLAND, as may be gathered by Ancient Histories, was by the **Phoenicians**, some say by *Hercules* ... long before the First *Olympiad* ... *Anno* 3938.' The classical Cassiterides were the Isles of Scilly and Cornwall, and Cornish tin was the objective of the Phoenician traders. The Hercules associated with Tyre in Greek mythology comes in here (as he had with Bochart) and Sammes, taking up Ptolemy's placename *Herculis promontorium* on the North Devon coast, brought him to Hartland Point. The Greeks followed up in the Cornish tin trade and they of course introduced Homeric chariot warfare. Despite what Bishop Nicolson and others had to say, Sammes was undoubtedly read, and his Phoenicians were to become a part of British archaeological folklore almost until today. Dr Plot in 1677, and apparently independently of Sammes publishing only the year before, also looked to the tin trade and to Greeks encountering Britons 'long before the Arrival of the *Romans*', but 'long before that they were known to the *Phoenicians*, and all the *Eastern* countries is plain out of *Strabo* and *Bochartus* . . . the Eastern *Merchants* trading hither for *Tin.*' Such views were to form the nucleus of William Stukeley's fantasy about the Druids and Patriarchal Christianity, so persuasive and pervasive in the romanticism of the later eighteenth century. Optimism was to take over, with the Ancient Briton ready to become a Noble Savage.

Now, before we come to consider what the early antiquaries made of the field monuments of prehistory which they encountered and described in the countryside, a couple of general points may be made. The feet of Aylett Sammes never came near to touching the ground of archaeological reality, and no artifacts or monuments interfere in his pursuit of the past from texts and his own exuberant imagination; many were to follow this method (or madness). John Aubrey and William Stukeley, the two great fieldworkers, appear to have been unconcerned with the problems and possibilities raised by the question of Britons using stone or bronze; for Aubrey the ancient people of Wiltshire 'knew the use of iron', Stukeley saw bronze axes only as Druidic mistletoe-cutters. Edward Lhuyd alone saw flint arrowheads, bronze rapiers, megalithic monuments and hillforts within the same frame of reference. The second and more general phenomenon that inhibited understanding up to the last century was the lack of interest by the antiquaries in the practical technology of craftsmanship that alone illuminates processes as varied as stone and metal working, the handling of massive stones and the practices of simple plough-agriculture and peasant farming. Here the difficulty was, of course, that of the contemporary social structure and the gulf set, and maintained on both sides, between the gentleman and the artisan. Certainly Aubrey recorded his regret that as a boy, 'I lived not in a city, e.g. Bristol, where I might have an accesse to watchmakers, locksmiths, etc.', and the young Stukeley when in London frequented the shops of the scientific instrument makers,[17] but clockwork and precision instruments represented the high technology of the period, and stood apart from the simpler skills. John Evelyn was honestly snobbish about it when he wrote to Boyle in 1659 excusing himself from completing a History of Trades partly because of the 'many subjections, which I cannot support, of conversing with mechanical capricious persons'.[18] The only gentlemen with a real knowledge of the crafts were perhaps the architects, themselves in the seventeenth century just emerging from the ranks of builders and masons.

The monuments: Stonehenge and megaliths

Of the monuments in the field which first attracted the attention of the antiquaries Stonehenge was the most obvious, having figured in medieval legends popularized by Geoffrey of Monmouth in the twelfth century and later, with the Merlin story, becoming recorded and even illustrated in fourteenth-century sources as a Wonder of Britain, on one occasion sharing the honours with the stone circle at Rollright and the Uffington White Horse.[19] The first objective record of Stonehenge is however that made by the Dutch artist Lucas de Heere, whom we saw in Chapter 3 making drawings of Ancient Britons in 1575, for he visited the monument, probably in 1568–9 with another Dutch artist, Joris Hoefnagel, and recorded the legend of the stones 'where they still stand, in this manner, as I myself have drawn them on the spot' in the form of an admirable watercolour view, like a low oblique air photograph.[20] The complicated relationship between this, the watercolour view by William Smith of 1588, the print signed '1575 R.F.' and the inferior copy of this in the 1600 edition of Camden, must be left on one side, but the text of the description of Stonehenge given by De Heere in his 1575 manuscript and that of Camden (who probably never saw the stones) in 1586, and following him Speed in 1614 or Stow in 1631, must draw on a common unidentified source. We are not surprised to find it records the bones of giants from the adjacent barrows, some of 'a giant as much as 12 feet tall', which sounds like Sir Thomas Elyot's giant of 1538. Giants were to make a spectacular appearance in the Stonehenge story in a manuscript extravaganza circulating in the 1660s, *A Fool's Bolt soon shott at Stonage*,[22] where the author quotes Elyot at length (in black-letter to give an air of antiquity and inaccurately, bringing the giant from near Salisbury to 'three or four miles from Stonage') and gives as his conclusion

My bolt is soon shott in this short conjecture, that **Stonage** was an old British triumphall tropicall temple erected to *Anaraith*, their Goddess of victory, in a bloody field there, wone, by illustrious *Stanengs* and his Cangick Giants, from K. *Divitiacus* and his *Belgae*.

This at least assigns Stonehenge to the Britons, as in another context had Edmund Bolton in 1624 – 'that STONAGE was a work of the BRITANNS, the rudeness it selfe perswades', but Bolton thought it the tomb of Boadicea.[22]

By the 1660s however, as we saw in Chapter 1, a controversy on Stonehenge was being waged on a high level. It was begun in 1620, when James I, staying on a royal progress with the Earl of Pembroke at Wilton, commanded Inigo Jones, then architect for Pembroke, to write an account of Stonehenge. Jones's account and plans of the monument were 'moulded off, and cast into a rude Form, from some few indigested notes' after his death by his relative and pupil John Webb in 1655.[23] The text starts from the quite reasonable standpoint, in terms of the pessimistic model of stone-using savages, that the Britons (or their Druids) could hardly be its builders, for

there is little likelyhood of any such matter, considering especially what the *Druids* were; also what small experience the *Britans*, anciently inhabiting this Isle, had in knowledge of what ever *Arts*, much lesse of building, with like elegancy and proportion, such goodly works as *Stoneheng*.

So far so good, but then Jones, as almost everyone except Webb was to agree, made a fool of himself by wrenching the Stonehenge plan into a pseudo-classical fantasy of architectural regularity and proclaimed the monument to be 'a work, built by the *Romans*, and they the sole *Founders* thereof' in a classical Order: 'of this Tuscan order, a plain, grave and humble manner of *Building*, very solid and strong, *Stoneheng* principally consists.' Jones (or Webb) did however make a sensible and practical observation

The same kind of stone whereof this *Antiquity* consists may be found, especially about *Aibury* in North-*Wiltshire*, not many miles from it, where not onely are Quarries of the like stone, but stones of far greater dimensions than any at *Stoneheng* may be had . . . As also, not far from the edge of Wiltshire, in the ascent from *Lamborn* to *Whitehorse Hill*, the like stones are daily discovered.

This a welcome comment from an architect who knew his building stones, and all the more so since from Camden's day the Stonehenge sarsens had from time to time been considered as artificial, and made of a sort of Druidical concrete.

In 1662 Jones was countered by Dr Walter Charleton, Physician to Charles II and an original Fellow of the Royal Society, in his *Chorea Gigantum* (which takes us back to the giants again) and has Stonehenge 'Restored to the DANES'.[24] Charleton fell into the trap we have already described, that of assuming that the monuments and antiquities set out by the Danish antiquary Ole Worm in his *Danicorum Monumentorum libri sex* (1643) and the catalogue of his *Museum Wormianum seu Historia rerum variorum* (1655) were, because found in modern Denmark, products of the historical Danes in England. Charleton's anonymous editor of the 1725 reprint of the *Chorea Gigantum* records that, 'The Doctor, dissatisfied with Mr Jone's Discourse, caus'd a Copy of it to be transmitted to Olaus Wormius, the celebrated Antiquary of *Denmark*, and Wormius return'd his Opinion of *Stone-Heng* in Several Letters to Dr Charleton.' As Worm died of the plague in 1654, and Jones's book was not published until a year later, there is an unexplained discrepancy here.[25] Charleton dedicated his book to Charles II, and in his commendatory poem prefixed to it John Dryden hails him, 'Among th'*Asserters* of free Reason's Claim', in the Royal Society tradition, together with Francis Bacon, William Gilbert, Robert Boyle, William Harvey and Sir George Ent. Charleton wrote that 'having diligently compared STONE-HENG with other Antiquities of the same kind, at this day standing in *Denmark*, and finding a perfect *Resemblance* in most, if not all particulars, observable on both Sides . . . I now at length conceive it to be Erected by the DANES, when they had this Nation in *Subjection*'. Nothing illustrated by Worm is of course remotely like Stonehenge. In 1664, John Webb replied with a turgid and very long-winded *Vindication* of Jones, which brought the controversy to a boring close.[26] Camden himself had been inclined to associate the Rollright stone circle with Rollo the Dane, as was Plot, who however was more persuaded by other views, as we shall shortly see.

MARE

CIMBRI CUM

REGIO

CIMMERIORUM

Sive

CIMBRORUM

Voiages i
With the
And Mou
Originally
Varied b

All which na
The

To wh

A Germa
Bei

MORINI

CIMBRI *divictis*
Gallis Roman migrant

Rodanus
Rodanum
Alpes Alpr

Italia Phe: Turia Sive
Calabria Calab:

Montes Pyrenaei
Perani

Crag
Carec

Tela
Tillini

Narona
Naron-
Oneum

Histus
Butna

Byzantium

Thas
Thale

Tarocon
Tarcon

WESTWARDS FROM ARARAT

20 The coming of the Cimbri from the Black Sea to the English Channel, as seen by
Aylett Sammes on his map of the dispersal of mankind after the Flood, 1676.

21 Watercolour drawing of the stones of Stonehenge, 'as I myself have drawn them on the spot', about 1568–9 by Lucas de Heere.

22 Stone circle at Rollright, drawn and engraved by Michael Burghers for Robert Plot's *Natural History of Oxford-shire* (1677).

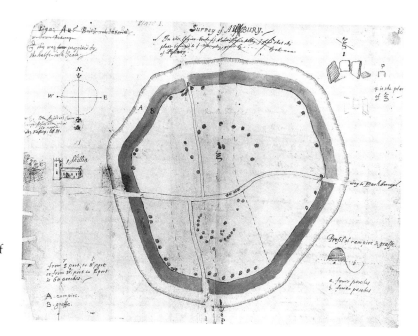

23 John Aubrey's
plane-table survey of
Avebury, originally
drawn to a scale of
half an inch to a
chain of 66 feet,
1663.

24 *(below)* William Stukeley's plan of Avebury drawn 1724 to about the same scale
as Aubrey's, with more detail but the earthwork shown inaccurately as a true circle.

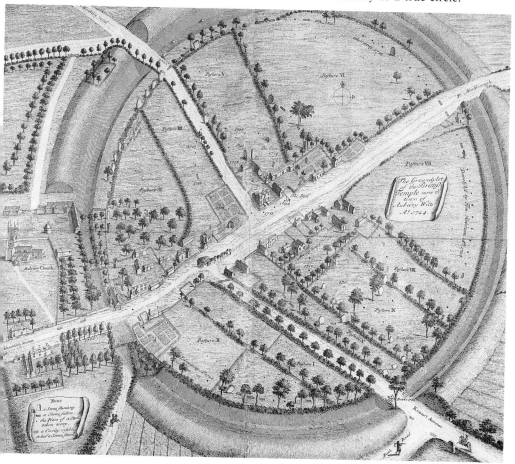

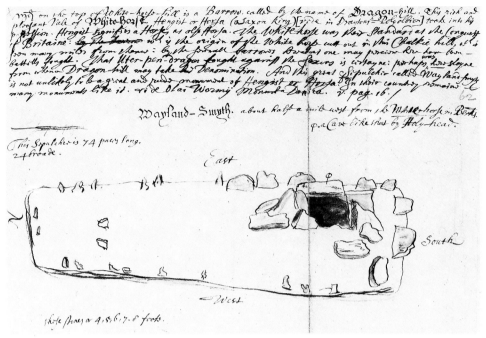

[Handwritten text in image:]

...on the top of White-horse-hill is a Barrow, called by the name of *Dragon-hill*. This rich and pleasant Vale of *White-Horse* Hengist or Horsa (a Saxon King) [vide in Drayton's Polyolbion] tooke into his possession. Hengist signifies a Horse, as also Horsa. The White-horse was their Standard at the Conquest of Britaine: by the... wch is the origin of the White horse cutt out in this Chalkie hill, it is seen many miles from thence: by the small barrows hereabout one may perceive here have been battells fought. That Uter-pen-dragon fought against the Saxons is certaine: perhaps here slayne from whence Dragon-hill may take its Denomination. And this great Sepulchre called Wayland-smyth is not unlikely to be a great and rude monument of Hengist or Horsa. In their country remaine many monuments like it. vide Olai Wormij monumenta Danica. v. pag. 16./

Wayland-Smyth. about half a mile west from the White-horse in Berks.
q. a Cave like this by Holy-head.

This Sepulchre is 74 paces long.
24 broade.

East

South

West

those stones a 4.5.6.7.8 foots.

25 Aubrey's unpublished plan of the chambered long barrow of Wayland's Smithy on the Berkshire Downs, from the *Monumenta Britannica*.

26 Drawing of Wayland's Smithy long barrow by W.Green for Francis Wise's *Letter to Dr Mead*, 1738.

WAYLAND-SMITH.

27 Stukeley's drawing of 1724 showing the Roman road cutting into an earlier (Bronze Age) disc barrow on Oakley Down, Dorset.

28 British gold coin of the first century BC showing a stylized and disjointed horse.

29 Air photograph of the chalk-cut White Horse of Uffington as it appears today.

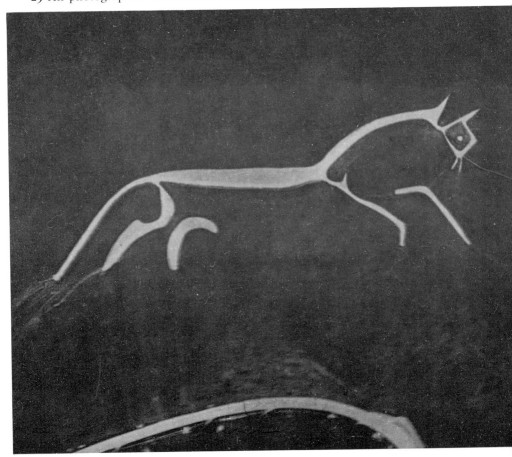

30 Detail of oil painting, *Le Singe Antiquaire*, by Jean Baptiste Chardin, 1740, showing a monkey, surrounded by numismatic publications, examining a coin with a magnifying glass.

31 *(above)* Watercolour b
Philip Crocker about 180
showing Colt Hoare and
William Cunnington
supervising the barrow-di
(probably John and Steph
Parker).

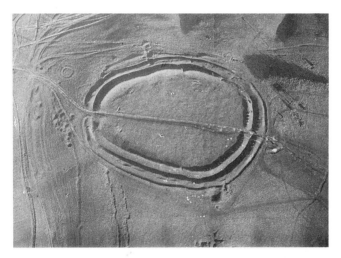

32 Air photograph of the
Age hillfort of Barbury C
Wiltshire.

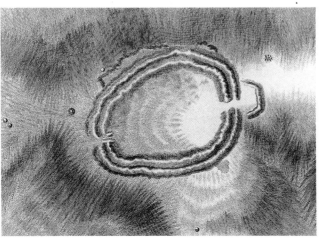

33 Plan by Philip Crocke
Barbury Castle hillfort as
engraved in the second v
of Colt Hoare's *Ancient
Wiltshire* (1821).

But by an odd quirk of fate it is to Charleton that we owe the impetus that resulted in the most important archaeological achievement of the seventeenth century, the *Monumenta Britannica* of John Aubrey. Aubrey, a Wiltshireman, had at the age of twenty-two first seen and recognized the importance of the great henge monument of Avebury at the end of a day's coursing on 6 January 1649 and later spent 'a week or two every Autumne' there. In 1663 he was elected an Original Fellow of the newly constituted Royal Society and had talked to his acquaintances there about the monument, saying 'that it did as much excell *Stoneheng* as a Cathedrall does a Parish church'. This was reported to Charles II in conversation about Stonehenge by the President of the Royal Society, Lord Brouncker (an Irish peer and mathematician whom Aubrey was not alone in regarding as 'a rotten-hearted false man') and Dr Charleton, whereupon the King, reported Aubrey, 'commanded Dr Charleton to bring me to him the next morning'. At the royal audience, to which Aubrey took a sketch plan of Avebury, the King asked him to show him the monument when he was on his way to Bath in a fortnight's time: this he did and, 'His Majestie then commanded me to give an account of the old Camps and Barrows on the Plaines'.[27] This royal command, recalling that of James I to Inigo Jones, was the beginning of the *Monumenta Britannica or a Miscellanie of British Antiquities*, a manuscript begun in 1663 but which Aubrey was never able to bring to completion; adding, deleting, altering and putting in new (and sometimes contradictory) ideas and notes over a period of more than thirty years, until 1694 or 1695. Despite the efforts of his friends in the early 1690s it was never published, so that its effect on contemporary scholars was largely indirect, or, as we shall see, through those parts published in Gibson's augmented edition of Camden's *Britannia* in 1695. Securing the use of the manuscript was a triumph for Thomas Tanner, a Wiltshireman and a contemporary of Gibson's at Queen's College Oxford, who took responsibility in 1693–4 for the Wiltshire portion of Camden. A brilliant young man (he was only twenty at the time) he must have had an engaging personality (in later life a contemporary described him as 'so extraordinarily a good Humoured person and so communicate that every one admires him') for he charmed Aubrey, slightly suspicious after his treatment by Anthony Wood over the *Brief Lives*, into lending his manuscript with permission to quote from it. When he saw it, Edmund Gibson as general editor (at the age of twenty-five!) was horrified, and wrote to Tanner

The accounts of things are so broken and short, the parts so much disorder'd, and the whole such a mere Rhapsody, that I cannot but wonder how that poor man could entertain thoughts of a present Impression.[28]

From the manuscript and the 1695 *Britannia* we can however piece together Aubrey's ideas on Stonehenge, Avebury and stone circles in general, on earthwork enclosures and hillforts, and on barrows.[29]

The core of Aubrey's projected work was an account of Avebury and Stonehenge with a few other stone circles, entitled *Templa Druidum* – indeed this was to have been the title of the whole book, but as it grew into a larger survey of antiquities including barrows and earthworks he altered this to *Monumenta Britannica*, following Ole Worm's *Monumenta Danica*, with the *Templa Druidum* as the first section. His first task was to make a remarkable plane–table survey of the Avebury circles, 'projected by the halfe-inch scale': no easy job with the village and its hedged enclosures to confuse the essential plan. If it somewhat exaggerates the irregularity of the layout, this is no less a fault than Stukeley's reduction of this to a geometrically accurate circle. Aubrey planned and described the stone circles of Stanton Drew (Somerset) in 1664, and in 1666 made a good sketch-plan of Stonehenge, the first of the monument except for Inigo Jones's 'Romanized' diagram, and noteworthy for recording depressions or 'cavities' within the bank, which led to their recognition and excavation in the 1920s as a circle of ritual pits of the first phase of Stonehenge, named the Aubrey Holes after his original discovery. He later added a dozen other stone circles from publications or information, such as Rollright (from Plot's 1677 *Oxfordshire*), the henges and stone circles of Arthur's Round Table, Mayborough and Long Meg from a manuscript of Dugdale's in the College of Arms, and some others over the years of tinkering with his own manuscript. But already in 1665, in a fair draft dated from Broad Chalk, he was able to write of stone circles

I am apt to believe, that in most Counties of England are, or have been Ruines of these kind of Temples . . . in the Kingdome of Ireland (especially in Ulster) are severall Monuments of the like nature

and is assured by many 'learned Gentlemen of Scotland . . . that in that Kingdom are severall Monuments of the Fashion before shewen.' He then makes his considered judgment.

Now to wind-up this Discourse. The Romans had no Dominion in Ireland or in Scotland at least not far: therefore these Temples are not to be supposed to be built by them: nor had the *Danes* Dominion in Wales: and therefore we cannot presume [two Welsh sites he had been told of] to have been Works of Them. But all these monuments are of the same fashion, and antique rudenesse: wherfore I conclude, that they were erected by the Britons: and were Temples of the Druids.

When Thomas Tanner was able to quote from the *Monumenta* in his additions to the 1695 *Britannia* he summed up Stonehenge and the current theories of its origin. ''Tis of it self so singular, and receives so little light from history, that almost every one has advanc'd a new notion... The opinions about it may be reduc'd to these 7 heads...' Of these seven the first is that of Sammes and the Phoenicians – 'a conjecture that has met with so little approbation, that I shall not stay to confute it'. Five others comprise the *Fools Bolt* and its giants, Bolton and Boadicea, Inigo Jones and the Romans, the medieval Uther Pendragon and British kings, the Danes (Charleton is not mentioned by name) and, second to the list,

That it was a Temple of the Druids long before the coming in of the Romans, which Mr *John Aubrey*, Fellow of the Royal Society, endeavours to prove in his Manuscript Treatise, entitle'd *Monumenta Britannica*.

Aubrey's hypothesis is clearly and fully acknowledged, but Tanner adds his own reservations. He can accept Stonehenge as British, but the sophistication of its architecture

makes it probable, that *Stonehenge* was built after the Romans came in, and in imitation of some of their structures, tho' as to the general part of the work, it appears to have been inartificial, and savours of their primitive rudeness.

Of Avebury, Tanner merely remarks that it is 'a monument more considerable in its self, than known to the world', quotes the *Monumenta* in the margin, and describes the main circles, the West Kennet avenue and the stone circles on Overton Hill later to be known as the Sanctuary, all from Aubrey's account.

But as we saw when dealing with the interpretation of prehistoric bronzes, Gibson had also secured the co-operation of Edward Lhuyd to revise the Welsh sections of the *Britannia*, which he did, in 1693–4.[30] Lhuyd knew Aubrey (who was to insert a transcript of the Pembrokeshire additions of 1695 into his *Monumenta*) and through him saw a group of letters of 1692–5 between Aubrey and Professor James Garden of Aberdeen on stone circles and the 'second sight'.[31] He was then able in his Pembrokeshire additions to refer to these and to Aubrey, 'an ingenious Gentleman of the Royal Society (who for what I can learn was the first that suspected these Circles for *Temples of the*

Druids)', after he had described the chambered tomb at Pentre Ifan, one of several sites he found called Cromlechs. These in contemporary folklore seemed to be associated with veneration or ceremonial, or as places of 'Idolatrous worship', and Garden had said the same of Scotland. Confusing chambered tombs and stone circles, Lhuyd thought 'our *Kromlech*, as well as all other such circular stone-monuments in Britain and Ireland (of which I presume there are not less than one hundred yet remaining) were also erected for the same use.' He then was to dispose of Dr Charleton's Danes – 'they will want History to prove, that ever the Danes had any Dominion, or indeed the least Settlement in Wales or the Highlands of Scotland, where such monuments are as frequent, if not more common, than in other parts of Britain.' The Danes were anyway marauders and raiders, and, says Lhuyd in a memorable phrase, 'such vast perennial memorials seem to be rather the work of people settled in their Country, than of such roving Pirates'. And as for the Scandinavian stone monuments illustrated by Worm and others, 'I find none of them comparable to that magnificent, tho' barbarous Monument on Salisbury Plain'. 'And I think it probable', Lhuyd concludes, 'should we make diligent enquiry, that there may be Monuments of this kind still extant in the less frequented places of Germany, France and Spain; if not also in Italy. But I fear I have too long detain'd the Reader with probabilities.' In 1699 he was in Ireland and wrote to Dr Tancred Robinson.

The most remarkable curiosity we saw by the way, was a stately Mount at a place called New Grange near Drogheda; having a number of huge stones pitch'd on end round it . . . a very broad flat stone, rudely carved . . . they discover'd to be the door of a cave, with a long entry leading to it . . . The great pillars round this cave . . . were not all hewn or wrought, but were such rude stones as those of Abury in Wiltshire, and rather more rude than those of Stonehenge.

A Roman coin of Valentinian had been found near the top of the mound, 'the coin proving it ancienter than any Invasion of the Ostmans or Danes; and the carving and rude sculpture, barbarous; it should follow that it was some place of sacrifice or burial of the ancient Irish'.[32] New Grange is one of the most famous of the megalithic chambered tombs of Europe, dated to 3175–3245 BC, and Lhuyd's assessment of its pre-Roman date and likely function embodied far more sound archaeological reasoning than the speculations of genera-tions to come.[33]

In considering megalithic monuments, Robert Plot turned to the work of young Edward Stillingfleet, aged twenty-seven, and later to be

Bishop of Worcester, the *Origines Sacrae* of 1662. His views on the ancient worship of standing stones caused Plot to seek for the Rollright Circle an alternative to Rollo and the Danes, an ancient British origin; such ideas 'especially as recommended by so learned a Person as the Reverend Dr *Stillingfleet*, have prevailed with me much'. He also quoted him in support of a similar attribution for the Devil's Arrows at Boroughbridge, a standing stone at Kinver in Staffordshire, the chambered tomb of Kit's Coty House in Kent, the Devil's Quoits at Stanton Harcourt in Oxfordshire, and Stonehenge itself.[34]

Earthworks and hillforts

The identification and classification of ancient bank-and-ditch enclosures, or those in rocky country with ruined stone walls, faced the early antiquaries with a problem which in the event they were unable to solve. As modern archaeologists know, without accurate survey and sophisticated excavation techniques developed only in the present century, surface distinction is still, with rare exceptions such as some Roman military works, impossible to make. The superficial appearance of an earthwork, from Leland and Camden onwards, could only lead to guesswork, and that within a misleading framework of literary evidence, which recorded three ancient peoples in Britain as builders of fortifications, successively the Romans, the Saxons and the Danes. When Leland said of the Wittenham Clumps hillfort in Berkshire that it was 'a castelle in the Britannes tyme' he was making an unusual and lucky guess, and Camden was more typical when he described in Dorset

A ditch with Bulwark on the top of an hill, pretty large in circumference, call'd Maiden Castle, which one may easily imagine to be the place where the Romans encamp'd in the summer time.

Military overtones were perceptible throughout – after all the use of the term 'camps' for prehistoric hill-top enclosures survives today – and owed much to the martial model presented by the Roman writers concerned with the conquest of Britain.

Edward Lhuyd was intending to discuss Welsh hillforts in his *Archaeologia Britannica* had he lived to write more than the first, philological, volume, planning, 'An Account of all such Monuments now remaining in *Wales*, as are presum'd to be *British*, and either older or not much later than the *Roman* conquest, viz. their Camps and Burial Places, the Monuments called *Cromlecheu and Meinieugwyr*

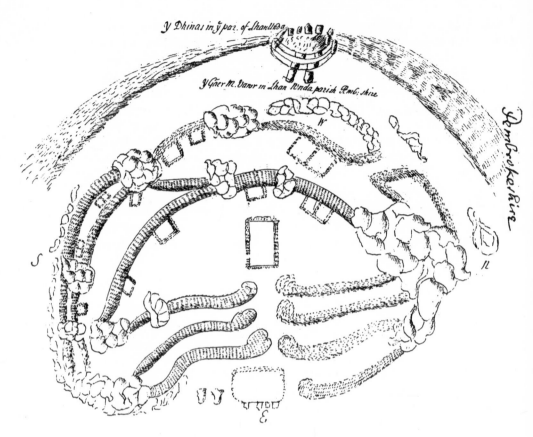

12 Plan of the hillfort of Y Dinas, Llanwnda, Pembrokeshire, made by William Jones for Edward Lhuyd 1697–8. It bears little resemblance to the actual site.

. . .'. In his *Britannia* contribution he notes in passing forts in Denbighshire, for example ('divers old Forts or Entrenchments in this County'), but of only one did he write that it 'was in all likelyhood a British camp, seeing it agrees exactly with Tacitus's description of the Camp of King *Caratacus*'. But for his own projected book he was getting hillfort plans made by his assistant William Jones, such as those of Pen-y-Gaer, Carnarvonshire and Y Dinas, Llanwnda, Pembrokeshire surviving among the antiquarian papers of the herald John Anstis.[35]

John Aubrey in his *Monumenta* followed the *Templa Druidum* section by one on 'Camps', which he dealt with at some length and with some pride at having achieved a classification. This started perfectly reasonably from the textual evidence that Roman forts and camps were normally quadrangular and constructed according to precise military specifications, Aubrey giving the classic statement of Polybius (VI, 27–32) by cutting out the relevant pages from a contemporary English translation and copying out the plan and description of a Roman fort from Sir Henry Savile's notes to his translation of Tacitus of 1591. Aubrey then gives sketch-plans and notes of a variety of earthworks, none rectilinear and none Roman (except the square temple on Farley Heath in Surrey). He is then wildly inconsistent. Of the Iron Age hillforts, for instance, in Hampshire, Quarley Hill is 'a great British camp' as opposed to the not far distant Danebury, 'a great Roman camp'. In Wiltshire indeed Sidbury is 'a great British camp' again, but Barbury Castle 'of British fashion: ? if Danish'. Badbury Rings in Dorset has 'double or treble Workes sc. Ramparts & graffes: therefore I assume it to be no Roman camp', as Aubrey seems to have taken multiple defences as a sign of at least non-Roman origin: Wandlebury near Cambridge is 'a British campe treble workt i [tem] three Rampires and two graffes between (as usually)'. A distinction he was proud to make was his least fortunate, that circular (or roughly round) earthworks were infallibly Danish. Of Figsbury Rings in Wiltshire he wrote, 'This was a Danish camp: as appears by its circular figure' and compares it with Chastleton in Oxfordshire, claimed as Danish by Plot in 1677, but 'he knew not how to distinguish a Rom: camp from a Danish till I told him'. Plot had set out his views with confidence

After the Departure of the *Romans* came the *Saxons* into *Britan,* and after them the *Danes,* who also made them works so indistinguishable from the *Romans* [apart from coin finds] that they can scarce be known asunder [so if they] have no *Roman Money,* I think we must conclude either *Saxon* or *Danish; Saxon* if square and if round *Danish* .. . as for *Chastleton Barrow,* by the above-mentioned *Rule,* it should be a Fortification of the *Danes.*

Thomas Tanner's contribution to the Wiltshire section of the 1695 *Britannia* ranks second to that of Lhuyd for amplitude and originality. In it he not only used material derived from Aubrey, but his own judgment, which in the instance of hillforts amounted to no more, as usual, than guesses. Figsbury, so securely Danish for Aubrey, was 'a very great entrenchment of a rude circular form . . . there is some probability of its being Saxon'. Sidbury appears as 'a vast fortification encompass'd with two deep ditches and of an oval figure ... It certainly appears to have been a Danish Camp' and Oldbury 'possibly Danish'.

Casterley Camp, Upavon, 'has but a single trench, and the name seems to point out to us something of Roman'. For prehistoric earthworks the utter confusion and ignorance of 1695 was to persist into the present century.

Barrows and cairns

Barrows thought of as burial monuments attracted attention in the Middle Ages as imagined repositories of treasure, and the royal exchequer, always with an eye to easy money, was alert to the legend, and royal commands to dig barrows for treasure go back to Henry III and barrows in Cornwall and the Isle of Wight in 1237, continuing elsewhere up to the seventeenth century. Sir John Oglander, who came to live in the Isle of Wight in 1607, soon interested himself in the local barrows but from the praiseworthy viewpoint of seeking not for treasure, but archaeological knowledge.

You may see [he wrote] divors buries on ye topp of owre Island hills whose name in ye Danische tounge signifieth theyr nature, as being places onlie weare men were buried ...I have digged for my experience in soome of ye moore auntientest, and have found manie bones of men formerlye consumed by fyor, according to ye Romane custome... Wheresoever you see a burie . . . digge and you shall find theyre bones.[36]

Sir John at least approached the problem empirically and experimentally, though one hopes his enthusiastic digging programme was not taken up. In the 1650s William Dugdale was much exercised with the problem of ancient tumulus burials, their date and the current assumption that barrows covered mass burials of those fallen in battle. He wrote to Dr Gerard Langbaine, an early experimental philosopher and Provost of Queen's College Oxford, to Edward Bysshe, Garter king of arms, and to Dr Thomas Browne of Norwich. Bysshe replied that 'upon the most diligent search into the Roman Storye I am yet able to make, I meet not with anything that comes any way home to your demand concerning the burying of Soldiers in the field.' Browne wrote an essay: 'Of artificial hills, mounts or burrows . . . what they are, to what end raised, and by what nations', deciding briefly that they could equally well be Roman, Saxon or Danish (he makes no mention of Britons) and suggests, more seriously than Oglander, the practical experiment of 'subterraneous enquiry by cutting through one of them either directly or cross-wise'.[37]

Lhuyd had intended to cover ancient 'Burial Places' in his own book, and in the 1695 *Britannia* mentions cairns and barrows in passing. In one instance, though, at a 'Barrow, call'd *Krig y Dyrn* in the Parish of *Tre'lech*' in Carmarthenshire, he caused an excavation to be made, exposing under a cairn

such a barbarous Monument as we call a *Kist-Vaen*, or *Stone-chest*, which was about four foot and a half in length, and about three foot broad . . . and considering the rudeness of the Monument describ'd, and yet the labour and strength requir'd in erecting it, I am apt to suspect it the Barrow of some British Prince, who might live probably before the Roman Conquest. For seeing it is much too barbarous to be suppos'd Roman, and that we do not find in History that the Saxons were ever concern'd here, or the Danes any farther than in plundering the Sea-coasts, it seems necessary to conclude it British.

Aubrey, characteristically, could not make up his mind, and with his magpie method in collecting notes and observations for the *Monumenta* could happily contradict himself. At one point he could write

The greatnesse and numerousnesse of the Barrows (the Beds of Honour where now so many Heroes lie buried in Oblivion) doe speak plainly to us, that Death and Slaughter once rag'd here, and that there were the Scenes, where terrible Battles were fought

and at another

I am not of the opinion, that all these barrows around Stonehenge were made for burying that were slayne hereabout in Battels: it would require a great deal of time and leisure to collect so many thousand loades of earth: and soldiers have something else to doe flagrante bello . . . So that I presume they were the Mausolea or Burying places for the great Persons and Rulers of those times.

Tanner, though he may have floundered unhappily among Roman, Saxon and Danish earthworks, when it came to barrows showed his sound sense. Describing the now destroyed Millbarrow near Avebury, a stone chambered long barrow with massive peristalith recorded by Aubrey and Stukeley, he writes that it is 'a large oblong barrow . . . environ'd with great stones about 6 or 7 foot high . . . As in this, so in all other circumstances, it is so like those *Wormius* describes, but it was the sepulcher of some Danish Commander.' For once, Worm's illustrations had helped rather than misled: the comparison is perfectly valid, for Worm does describe and depict Danish chambered tombs with long mounds and stone settings which are analogues to those of the British Neolithic series. As to round barrows in Wiltshire, Tanner, always scrupulous in acknowledging in text or margin his debt to Aubrey, produces an unattributed scheme of objective classification which must be his own. Noting that Camden after describing Silbury makes a digression about *Barrows*, we may also take notice there are several sorts of these upon these *Downs*. 1. Small circular trenches with very little elevation in the middle. 2. Ordinary barrows. 3. Barrows with ditches round them. 4. Large oblong barrows, some with trenches round them, others without. 5. Oblong barrows with stones set up all round them.

This concise and perceptive typology of the outward characteristics of Wessex barrows was that to be used by field archaeologists until modern times: re-stated as disc barrows, bowl barrows, bell barrows, unchambered long barrows and megalithic chambered long barrows it remained the textbook classification into the 1930s and beyond. Tanner was to have a distinguished career as an ecclesiastical historian and churchman; described by a modern scholar as 'one of the most erudite members of a learned church'[38] he ended his career as Bishop of St Asaph. His work on the *Britannia* suggests that in his youth he also had the makings of an archaeologist of some quality.

John Aubrey died in 1697, Edward Lhuyd in 1709; Tanner and Gibson, both Bishops, in 1735 and 1740. With the close of the seventeenth century, British antiquarian and nascent archaeological studies came to the end of an epoch. Ten years before Aubrey's death William Stukeley was born, a complex character who was on the one hand to take up Aubrey's work as a field archaeologist of great distinction, and on the other to mislead generations as the inventor and propagator of a fantastic past for ancient Britain, dominated by fictitious Druids. With Stukeley it is appropriate to begin a new chapter, but the seventeenth century and its antiquarianism may have an apt valediction in the inimitable prose of Sir Thomas Browne. At the end of his essay on barrows that he sent to Dugdale he wrote, after a jejune enough statement of his views (for it was in 1658, the year in which he commemorated urn burial in the majestic and sonorous cadences of *Hydriotaphia*):

Surely many noble bones and ashes have been contented with such hilly tombs; which neither admitting ornament, epitaph or inscription, may, if earthquakes spare them, out-last all other monuments. *Suae sunt metis metae.* Obelisks have their term, and pyramids will tumble, but these mountainous monuments may stand, and are like to have the same period with the earth.

5

Relapse, romantics and stagnation

By the beginning of the eighteenth century the ancient Briton had emerged as an object of study no longer related to the Biblical narrative except in the vague sense of being the ultimate descendant of Noah, Japhet and Gomer, a matter of more consequence to philologists seeking, however ineffectually, the origins of language, than to the student of ancient monuments or artifacts –

> those learned philologists who trace
> A panting syllable through time and space,
> Start it at home, and hunt it in the dark
> To Gaul, to Greece, and into Noah's Ark.[1]

For those making what was to become an archaeological approach to the past, the Hanoverian Latitudinarian Church presented no opposition to intellectual enquiries pursued along rational lines and indeed was to a large degree doctrinally based on such a world-view.[2]

The Anglican church, with a sense of relief and indeed weariness, after the religious controversies culminating in the mid-seventeenth century, had adopted an unadventurous but comfortably undemanding stance in which the harmony and order of the universe, as demonstrated mathematically by Newton, supported by the enquiries of the natural philosophers, could only imply a wise and beneficent Creator who in his world displayed *The Wisdom of God Manifested in the Works of the Creation*, as the title of Ray's book of 1691 proclaimed. This manifestation, essentially for man's delight, was a simple demonstrative faith which could be apprehended and understood by reason, with its divine nature further supported and validated by an again uncomplicated revelation of God to man, especially in the fulfilment in the New Testament of the prophecies of the Old, and by its miracles including the Resurrection. As set out, for instance, in Dr Samuel Clarke's much esteemed Boyle Lectures for 1704–5, *The Being and Attributes of God*, one sees the dangers of the more simplistic aspect of Latitudinarianism and its comprehensive tolerance. On the one hand there were the inbuilt dangers latent in doctrinal vagaries such as Arianism (from the third century: Christ not 'consubstantial' with God) or Socinianism (from the sixteenth century: Christ not Divine) which could easily lead to Deism, in which all revelation was questioned or rejected. One of the earliest and most pungent protagonists of Deism was John Toland. He, with William Stukeley as a Church of England opponent, brought antiquarianism into religious controversy when they both concerned themselves with Druids derived from John Aubrey's innocuous comments. This, as we shall see, had momentous results for the concept of prehistoric Britons. The Latitudinarian position on the other flank, was vulnerable, by its insistence on a rational Christianity, to the attacks of the dissenting sects and others who placed a higher value on revelation and individual inspiration. It was the Latitudinarian Joseph Butler, author of the famous *Analogy of Religion* (1736) who, as Bishop of Bristol, reprimanded John Wesley in 1739: 'Sir, the pretending to extraordinary revelations and gifts of the Holy Ghost is a horrid thing – a very horrid thing.' The latent polarity of thought and emotion was to find expression in the Agnostics and the Evangelical Church of the nineteenth century, with their repercussions on geology and archaeology.

Stukeley the field archaeologist

For the moment we can put religion, Druids and enthusiasm aside, turn to Stukeley, and consider his contribution to field archaeology before he so unfortunately brought ancient Britons and religious controversy together. William Stukeley (1687–1765) is a remarkably well-documented figure who has been the subject of a recent biographical study by the writer.[3] He was educated as a physician in Cambridge and in London at St Thomas's Hospital under Dr Richard Mead, 1703–10, when he took a practice in his native Lincolnshire for seven years before he returned to London. By this time he had begun to make tours of the countryside with his friends: in 1710 to Northamptonshire, Oxford and the Rollright stone circle, in 1712 as far afield as Wales, through the Derbyshire Peak district, Manchester and Chester to Wrexham. The Tour was becoming popular, with the redoubtable Celia Fiennes travelling indefatigably throughout Britain in 1685–

1705, and in 1725 Daniel Defoe began writing up his extensive travels made in the previous years.[4] Stukeley's tour journals, later to be published in his *Itinerarium Curiosum* of 1724, show at first no more than the ordinary slight antiquarian interest any gentleman of his time might have shared, though later they become more directly archaeological. But already in 1716 his attention had turned to the monument of Stonehenge, which, with Avebury, was in one way or another to form the pivot of his intellectual life for the next thirty years. 'Happening to fall' he wrote to a friend in June 1716

into a set of thoughts about Stonehenge in Wiltshire, by a prospect of Loggan's which I met withall, I undertook to make an exact Model of that most noble and stupendous piece of Antiquity, which I have accomplish'd, and from thence drawn a groundplot of its present ruins, and the view of it in its pristine State . . . and propose from thence to find out . . . its design, use, Founders etc . . .

How he managed to deduce the plan of Stonehenge from the two admirable landscape views engraved by David Loggan (1635–93) is a mystery: the only actual plans to which he could have had access would be those of Inigo Jones, Webb and Charleton already discussed. However, by 1717–19, his interest in Stonehenge was to be reinforced by a far more potent influence.

Soon after his return to London he had begun what was to be a life-long friendship with the brothers Roger and Samuel Gale, both interested in antiquities and sons to the great Restoration scholar Thomas Gale, Regius Professor of Greek at Cambridge until 1672 when he resigned to become High Master of St Paul's School in London, until 1697 when he became Dean of York. He knew Aubrey, who stayed with him in London in 1692–94 when he was corresponding with Professor Garden of Aberdeen on stone circles and who refers to him as 'my faithful friend'. Thomas Gale was an historian who edited Gildas and Nennius as well as the Antonine Itinerary of Roman Britain, published posthumously by his son Roger in 1709, and made an annotated transcript of much of Aubrey's *Monumenta Britannica* manuscript (including the *Templa Druidum* section). This must have been lent by Roger Gale to Stukeley, who re-transcribed it on thirty-eight pages of a folio note-book, ending 'Thus far Mr Gale's Notes out of Mr Aubrey's Collections 10 Dec 1718 W.S.' In the next year he similarly made notes from manuscripts of Edward Lhuyd's dealing with stone circles and megalithic monuments in England, Wales, Scotland and Ireland, occupying another thirty-four pages, 'from Mr E. Lhwyd's MS Sept 1719 . . . in the hands of Mr Anstis Garter King of

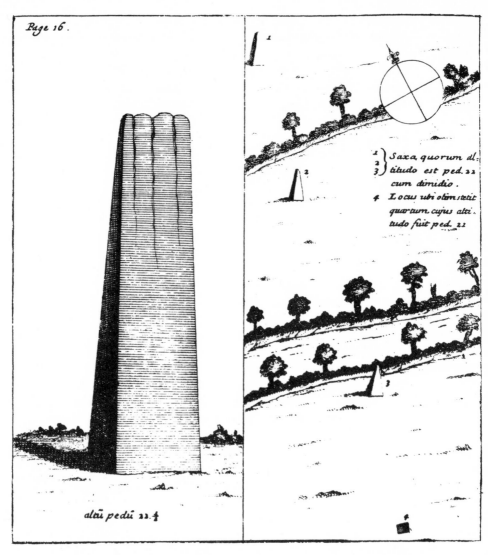

altũ pedũ 22.4

1
2
3 } Saxa quorum al-
titudo est ped. 22
cum dimidio.

4 Locus ubi olim stetit
quartum, cujus alti-
tudo fuit ped. 22

13 Standing stones known as The Devil's Arrows, Boroughbridge, West
Yorkshire. Engraving in Thomas Gale, Antonini Iter Britanniarum, edited
by his son Roger, 1709.

Arms'. John Anstis (1669–1744), was a herald who collected two volumes of notes and drawings on antiquities including stone circles and plans made for Lhuyd of hillforts, as we saw: neither the Gale transcript of the *Monumenta* nor it seems the Lhuyd manuscript lent by Anstis to Stukeley has survived.[5] But by May 1719 Stukeley had gone with Roger and Samuel Gale to make his first visits to Avebury and Stonehenge. His life-work as a student of ancient Britain was now determined.

In his writing Stukeley makes only passing references to Aubrey, his ideas on stone circles and Druids, or to knowledge of the *Monumenta* and the Lhuyd manuscripts. It must be admitted that, though outstanding as a field archaeologist, he was no scholar. In his published books there is a singular scarcity of references to other people's work, in a manner very different from, for instance, the abundantly documented pages of Plot. In the preface to his *Stonehenge* volume of 1740 he writes, rather ingenuously, 'the method of writing, which I have chosen is a diffusive one, not pretending to a formal and stiff scholastic proof of everything I say, which would be odious and irksome to the reader, as well as myself'; in the *Itinerarium Curiosum* of 1724 he says that he has a 'long and particular catalogue' of Roman coins from Castor, 'but think it a nauseous formality to print 'em'. But his silence on his debt to Aubrey is more than carelessness, and must have been prompted by a wish to claim the credit for first recognizing the importance of Avebury, Stonehenge and allied monuments as an unacknowledged result. The Deist John Toland, whose doctrines he would attack in the 1740s, was writing on Druids and stone circles to Lord Molesworth with full recognition of Aubrey (whom he had known); essays only to be published in 1726.

However chary he may have been in acknowledging his indebtedness to Aubrey's work as its impetus, Stukeley's fieldwork at Avebury and Stonehenge was an outstanding *tour de force*. From 1719 to 1724 he spent up to two months at a time between May and August, making notes, theodolite surveys and perspective drawings not only as exact and detailed records but, to a degree unshared by his contemporaries, with a keen awareness of making descriptions of the monuments for posterity in advance of imminent destruction by intensified agriculture and building development. At Stonehenge he wrote, he was at pains to 'perpetuate the vestiges of this celebrated wonder & of the barrows avenues cursus &c for I forsee that it will in a few years be universally plowd over and consequently defacd.' At Avebury the sarsen stones were newly being broken up for building blocks by fire and water – 'the

O qui me gelidis in vallib'Hæmi | Atq3 metus Omnes & inexorabile Fatum
Siſtatꝗ ingeuti ramorum protegat umbra! | Subjecit pedibus, ſtrepitumꝗ Acherontis
Fœlix qui potuit Rerum cognoſcere cauſas! | avari. Virg.

14 *William Stukeley's title-page for his unpublished book on Avebury and Stonehenge written in 1723. The quotation is from Virgil, Georgics II, 488–92.*

barbarous massacre of a stone here with leavers and hammers, sledges and fire, is as terrible a sight as a Spanish Atto de fe . . . the faggots, the smoak, the prongs, and squallor of the fellows looks like a knot of devils grilling the soul of a sinner.'

This incomparable fieldwork represents the culmination of the Royal Society tradition of empirical observation and record, unfortunately achieved at a time when the Society had first become, under Newton's over-long presidency from 1703–1728, almost entirely mathematical in its interests, and latterly in general intellectual decline. Stukeley was alone, now old-fashioned as a representative of a standard of antiquarian scholarship higher than that in which he found himself. It was in this worthy tradition that at Avebury in July 1723 he settled down and drafted a book, *The History of the Temples of the Ancient Celts*, for which he drew a decorative title-page. Before turning to its content, the title demands a short comment. In it Stukeley is one of the first to use 'Celts' as an alternative to 'Britons' for a prehistoric people. While a recognition that the Gauls and the Britons were in some sense related went back to Camden and Verstegen, and Lhuyd had settled the linguistic affinities of what he was firmly calling 'Celtic languages' by the late 1690s, the concept of Gauls and Britons as Celts was only grasped after Yves Pezron published his *L'Antiquité de la Nation et de la Langue des Celtes* in 1703, with a translation by David Jones in 1706 in which the '*Celtae* or *Gauls*' are 'taken to be originally the same People as our *Ancient Britons*'.[6]

To return to the draft book of 1723. It is in two parts each in a separate MS volume, now respectively in Oxford and Cardiff,[7] the first part, with the title-page, being a description of Avebury prefaced by a general review 'of the Manner of Celtic Temples', taken basically from the Aubrey transcript with additions for Wales from Lhuyd's 'additions to Camden' and Ireland from his MSS, for Scotland Martin Martin's *Description of the Western Islands* . . . (1703) and James Wallace's *An Account of the Islands of Orkney* (1693). This survey occupies forty-eight folios and is followed by a description of Avebury

I shall take the reader a fine tour along with me quite round the verge of the temple but how much more agreeable upon the spot tho' accompany'd with the trouble of climbing over the hedges . . . the particularity of this description is designed to preserve the memory of this most illustrious Work of the highest Antiquity, & writing it upon the Spot made me catch at every appearance that I thought tended that way & had a regard in the eye of the Founders. If it be not too dry for the entertainment of the present Age it may assist in their contemplation of what reality remains & I hope will tempt them strictly to survey it, which may rescue some part from impending ruin when the Countrey finds an advantage in preserving its poor reliques, but future times may hence be able to ascertain its purport, when this sort of learning will be more cultivated.

These brave words were not to be printed, but much of the manuscript was destined to become the text of the *Abury* volume Stukeley published in 1740, and a total of at least ninety-four folios have been cut out or cancelled, but the latter part of the volume, some fifty pages, is intact, dealing with Egyptians, Cabiri, Corybants, Oscophoria and Tympana and other matters relating to ritual such as might be practised at henge monuments. Druids receive no more than a passing mention.

The Stonehenge volume, titled as Part II, and also dated 1723, opens

Great as were the Conceptions of the Founders of Abury, yet Stonehenge is not ashamed to claim the second Place to it. its materials are not altogether so extravagant in bulk, but its neatness & improved Ornament with Drayton in his Polyolbion well entitles it First Wonder of our Land . . . That the same People founded both, was there any room to scruple I shall show . . . in that way they were built by the same measure which I call the Celtic foot.

This last is crossed out, and 'cubit' substituted in a later hand: the cubit was to be the Druidic and Patriarchal measurement. For the rest, as with Avebury he takes the reader on a conducted tour of the landscape, barrows, cursus and avenue to the monument itself. A remarkable section, 'Enginry' contains a very practical and sensible discussion of how the Stonehenge structure could have been erected by the use of sledges, rollers, timber cradles and levers, in a manner not to be visualized until modern times. Had the 1723 book been published as we have it in manuscript, Stukeley's reputation would have been very different from that based on what was in fact to appear in 1740 and 1743. We must turn later to this; for the present we can further examine his fieldwork as shown not only in his Avebury and Stonehenge campaigns but as it appears in his *Itinerarium Curiosum* of 1724.

The tours which make up the book were undertaken over four or five years, from before 1710 to 1724 and although edited for the final printed text, seem to retain something of his developing ideas over this period. Stone circles such as Rollright or Stanton Drew he mentions only to refer the reader to his forthcoming separate account (the 1723 draft of course), but in the manuscript of the *Iter Oxoniense* (1710) which survives, he had said of the Rollright stones, 'I cannot but

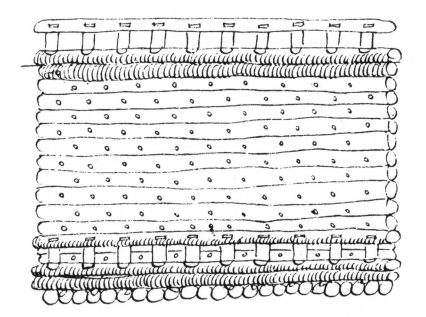

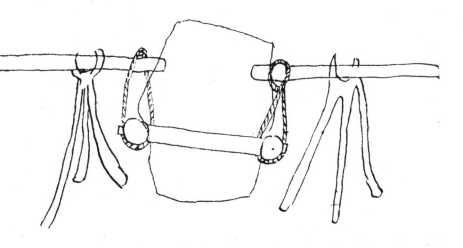

15 *Drawings from Stukeley's section on 'Enginry' in his 1723 MS,
showing timber framework (top) and lifting by levers (above) of the
Stonehenge stones.*

suppose 'em to have been a heathen temple of our Ancestors, perhaps in the Druids' time'. In the printed version of 1724 this appears as 'the first antiquity of this sort that I had seen, and from which I concluded to be temples of the antient *Britons*'. He had presumably read Tanner's remarks on Wiltshire barrows in the 1695 *Britannia* and does not elaborate on their classification, but is consistent in calling them 'Celtic' – near Rollright is 'a curious barrow neatly turn'd like a bell, small and high. I believe it *celtic*'. Of a long barrow near Dunstable, 'I have no scruple in supposing it *celtic*', and near are round barrows, a 'number of barrows or *celtic tumuli*'; on Brimpton Common (Berks) are 'many very fine *celtic* barrows' and so on. Near Beckhampton in Wiltshire and on Oakley Down in Dorset he made his classic observations that disc barrows were cut into by Roman roads, and at the latter site described the tumulus as 'one form of these barrows for distinction sake I call *druid* (for what reasons I shall not stand here to dispute) are thus, a circle of 100 foot diameter more or less . . .' with further details of a typical disc barrow, Tanner's first type, but the Druid attribution is, in his airy way, left unsubstantiated. Two undated MS schemes of his, 'The form of the barrows at Stonehenge in section' and 'Celtic sepulchral monuments at Abury' include 'Druids', 'Druid & his wife', 'King of Ancient Form', 'King and his Friend', 'Arch-druids, long' and so on for a couple of dozen varieties.[8] King Barrow above Wilton (Wilts) he regards as 'a grave of a king of this country of the Belgae . . . questionless a *celtic tumulus*' and has a private in-joke for Lord Pembroke and the Society of Roman Knights by attributing it to Carvilius, Pembroke's nickname in the society. The battle-barrows of Dugdale and Browne have gone: 'Quite otherwise; they are assuredly, the single sepultures of kings, and great personages, buried during a considerable space of time, and that in peace'. His barrow excavations near Stonehenge, carried out at Pembroke's instigation, were superior in recording to many we know of until the nineteenth century, but the 'considerable space of time' does not seem, if we are to go by Carvilius, to date much before Caesar's time. Believing the ancient Britons to have a knowledge of the magnetic compass he, with the assistance of his friend the Astronomer Royal, Edmond Halley in the 1740s, who misinterpreted the then available evidence for magnetic variation, later calculated that the bearing of the axis of Stonehenge indicated a date of 460 BC. By a wholly unjustified extrapolation from this fictitious date he put Avebury at 1860 BC, neatly conforming with Ussher's date for Abraham.

When we come to Stukeley's observations on earthworks and

hillforts we make no advance over earlier guesswork, except that, mercifully, the Danes are gone. On three or four occasions he thought hillforts might be pre-Roman: 'on the eastern side of *Enfield* chace close by *Bush-hill* is a circular *british* camp upon an eminence'; at Harbury Banks, Ashwell in Hertfordshire 'tho' *roman* coynes have been found in it, I am inclinable to think 'tis earlier than their times', and at Maiden Bower (Beds) 'I'm persuaded 'tis a *british* work like that at Ashwell'. And surprisingly in Wiltshire he describes the fine fort of Tisbury Castle Ditches as 'a great entrenchment in a wood which was probably a *british oppidum*', and at Ogbury 'I doubt not this was a camp of the *Brittons*', whereas all the other forts are, like Yarnbury, 'a vast *roman* camp' Figsbury, a 'famous *roman* camp; Oldbury a 'great and strong *roman* camp', and in Dorset, Maiden Castle was 'undoubtedly the Aestiva of the Durnovarian garrison . . . its manner savoring of inferior times of the empire'. As to the linear earthworks of Wessex, from Comb's Ditch to Wansdyke, Stukeley followed Aubrey, who thought them British boundaries in tribal warfare. There is clearly no new contribution here.

Where Stukeley did make original observations was in the recognition of prehistoric field systems. Inside the Ogbury hillfort (which as we saw he thought 'British') he recorded

many little banks, carry'd strait and meeting one another at right angles, square, oblong parallels and some oblique, as the meres and divisions between plow'd lands; yet it never seems to have been plow'd.

and in Dorset on Cranborne Chase

I frequently observ'd on the sides of hills long divisions very strait crossing one another with all kinds of angle, they look like the baulks or meres of plow'd lands, and are really made of flint oregrown with turf: they are too small for plow'd lands, unless of the most ancient *Britons*, who dealt little that way.

Two things hindered comprehension, the concept of ancient Britons as non-agricultural hunters, and the modern landscape of the open field system of midland England in which he travelled. However, he objectively described the phenomenon, to be ignored or misinterpreted from his day to Cunnington around 1800.

The coins of the ancient Britons

The recognition of a native coinage among the immediately pre-Roman Iron Age Britons was one of the achievements of William

Camden. John Leland, who had numismatic contacts as a young man in Guillaume Budé, did not accept this, but Camden was objective and unequivocal. 'There are now and then found in this Island', he wrote, 'gold, silver and brass coins, of several shapes and weight; most of them hollow on one side: some without letters, others with letters curiously wrought', and among the abbreviated inscriptions such as CVNOB and CAMV, VER, BODVO, COM and REX CALLE he rightly recognized the names of historical persons, such as Cunobelin and Commius, places such as Camulodunum and Calleva, attributable to the pre-Roman kingdoms of south-east England known from the classical sources. He considered the function of the coins as currency: 'whether this sort of money went commonly currant in the way of trade and exchange, or was at first coined for some particular use, is a question among the learned', and decided that some sort of tribute or taxation was likely. 'But whether this Tribute-money was coined by the Romans or their Provincials, or their Kings . . . I cannot easily tell. One may guess them to have been stamp'd by the British Kings.' Modern numismatists agree with Camden. Issued by native chiefs or paramount chiefs such as Cunobelin from mints such as Camulodunum, 'the likelihood is that coinage was first required for such purpose as tribute, taxes, fines, dowries and offerings, rather than for transactions in the market place'.[9] Camden illustrated coins from the collection of Sir Robert Cotton, and in the 1695 edition a total of seventy-two were illustrated, augmented from Speed, Plot and Thoresby, with a few not ancient British, and an uninformative commentary by Obadiah Walker (1616–99), Master of University College Oxford from 1676, a post from which he was ejected in 1689 following his public acceptance of the Roman Catholic faith on the accession of James II.

William Stukeley in his early years developed an interest in British coins which was to continue throughout his life.[10] His first notebook on the subject is titled, 'Brittish coins drawn by Wm Stukeley 1720' and further notes continue into the 1760s. One of the first projects for the new Society of Antiquaries, founded in 1717, and at the instigation of Stukeley as its first Secretary, was

to attempt a Compleat Description and History of all the Coyns relating to Great Britain from the Earliest times to our own. Wm Stukeley undertook the British Coyns in Sir Hans Sloan's Cabinet or elsewhere.

as the Society's minutes for 3 January 1721/22 record. Stukeley in a later retrospective account wrote:

We founded the Antiquarian Society. Soon after we order'd a Committee to consider the antient coins pertaining to the Kingdom . . . the *British* was enjoined to me. I have never since lost sight of the Inquiry . . . I have made innumerable drawings of all the *Brittish* coins in Sr Hans Sloans Collection, Ld Pembroke, Winchelsea & others, wherever I cd. find them.

His drawings of coins and his notes of their provenances have a lasting value: as Derek Allen said in his sympathetic study, 'His writings as a numismatist, with all their defects, were intended as a step in the right direction. Moreover, in the notebooks, and particularly that of 1720, he has saved from oblivion the origins and pedigrees of a great many important British coins.' But unfortunately (and inevitably) he could not accept Camden's wise assessment of their economic function in Celtic society. Stukeley persuaded himself that an essential feature of the ceremonies at Stonehenge and other henge monuments was chariot-racing along the elongated earthwork enclosures he therefore designated *cursus* or race-tracks and concluded that the coins (themselves after all so often depicting horses and chariots) were the prizes at such contests – 'But observe we', he wrote, 'rude as they are, there is the use and purpose of our coins sufficiently evident, in the barriers for the horse and chariot races, where they were the victors rewards.' For Stukeley, too, the coins attested the civility of the ancient Britons, and to an optimistic rather than a pessimistic view of primitive culture. In the 1760s he wrote of the coins

When we consider them to be truly *Brittish*, as found only in *Brittain*, in such quantities, one wd. wonder how mankind cd. so easily be led, one after another, into the idle notion of the old Britons being a wild, uncultivated people; such as we find in the West Indies. I call it, an idle notion, bec. tis for want of thought, & reasoning, that we entertain it, & merely bec. writers, one after another, tell us so.[11]

To sum up, Stukeley's main contribution to British prehistoric archaeology, the detailed surveys of Avebury and Stonehenge, were contained in the unpublished manuscript of 1723, from which he extracted, in 1740 and 1743, the factual content of his two published books on the monuments, embedding them in a strange mixture of speculation and fantasy on Druids and Patriarchal Christianity. Before that, the *Itinerarium* stood as his sole antiquarian publication, in which (with it must be admitted some rather light-weight topography in the manner of the day) were included some sound archaeological observations. His attribution of long and round barrows as individual graves of important people in a prehistoric 'Celtic' past was an advance over the battle-barrows of vague antiquity previously favoured, but had been anticipated by Lhuyd; Stukeley demonstrated their pre-Roman date by observing their relationship to Roman roads as Lhuyd had used the Roman coin at Newgrange. So far as earthworks and hillforts are concerned, Stukeley's guesses were no better than Aubrey's, except for the exclusion of the Danes. His recognition of prehistoric field-systems was new, and important. On the whole his work, always excepting the unpublished Avebury and Stonehenge surveys, is no more than a worthy text to set beside those of Aubrey, Tanner and Lhuyd in the 1690s, carried out and presented to the public thirty years later, and in a world of learning which had sadly changed.

Decline

There is no need here to labour the point so often made by historians of 'the general lethargy which overtook European science soon after 1700'. The last of the great Restoration historians died between 1710 and 1740; for some seventy years after 1705 'the Earth-sciences lay stagnant and forgotten'; in palaeontology 'England became an intellectual backwater soon after the beginning of the century'.[12] In antiquarianism and early archaeology as it was emerging in Restoration times, the same can be seen to have taken place, and Stukeley old-fashioned and out-of-date by reason of his continuation of work to standards of a more worthy past. Increasingly an isolated figure, he was perhaps unconsciously under pressure to draw attention to himself and his work in increasingly bizarre speculations, as the sober presentation of facts proved no longer of interest to readers, and so to the booksellers.

The Reverend Francis Wise, of Trinity College Oxford, has earned the gratitude of posterity by his organizing (with Thomas Warton) the award of an honorary MA of the University for Samuel Johnson in 1755, just in time for it to appear on the title-page of the great Dictionary. Born in Oxford in 1695, Wise was an assiduous university politician who obtained for himself the appointment of Bodley's Sub-Librarian in 1719, that of Keeper of the University Archives in 1726, a couple of church livings, and finally in 1748 the desirable sinecure of Radcliffe Librarian, in James Gibbs's grand new building, 'little cumbered by books and almost entirely unencumbered by readers', a post he held to the end of his life in 1767. Wise was early interested in history and antiquities, and in 1722 published an unscholarly text of Asser's Life of King Alfred and, with his interest aroused by the battle of Ashdown and Alfred's defeat of the Danes in

871, surprisingly undertook a few days' fieldwork on the Berkshire Downs to examine and record the antiquities there, in 1738. His main concern was with the Uffington White Horse, which he regarded as a memorial to Alfred's victory, and he published his observations as *A Letter to Dr Mead, concerning some Antiquities in Berkshire* . . . , the distinguished physician Richard Mead under whom Stukeley had trained as a young man at St Thomas's.[13]

Wise opens his little pamphlet with a review of antiquarian studies in the 1730s as he saw them. 'The study of our national antiquities has till of late wanted the encouragement, which it deserved . . . The dislike often expressed for the study of Antiquities, might however more easily be born, if it proceeded only from those, who are at enmity with learning in general . . . But to hear this sort of Learning decried by gentlemen well versed in other branches of knowledge, is to *Receive wounds in the house of our friends*.' But, Wise goes on, the publication of the 1695 *Britannia* set things on a new foundation, and 'young gentlemen have been taught to reckon this study their chiefest personal accomplishments', though one wonders who the young gentlemen could have been. So too, 'A Society of Antiquaries has been formed, whose united endeavours, promise not only, to bring to light thousands of new particulars, relating to our English History, but correct the falsities of as many old ones.' As we saw, the Society was founded in 1717, and by the 1720s its first secretary, William Stukeley, was not so sanguine as Wise. He was not a Fellow until 1749, and he thought it would be useful if 'the most knowing members would form themselves into small parties, each party at their leisure undertaking a distinct province and in the nature of a travelling Committee' make records of local antiquities. Such research was not to the liking of the early Fellows, as the failure of the committees on coins showed.

Under a sub-heading British Antiquities, Wise sums up current knowledge 'of our more early History and antiquities'. 'If any part was obscure, the British must have been remarkably so: the times preceding Julius Caesar's invasion being a dark, and impenetrable, wild, without letters and almost without monuments, save what later antiquaries have discovered to belong to it.' But 'the rites and customs of the Druids have been traced out more curiously than heretofore'. Stonehenge is 'universally allowed to be a British Temple' together with Avebury and Rollright, 'of all which and more we may expect still a much better account, from a very learned and celebrated pen.' Here a footnote directs us to 'Dr Stukely', who though in 1738 he had not yet published his Avebury and Stonehenge books, had evidently convinced the learned world in conversation of his authority in such matters. 'I cannot think that any branch of our Antiquities has received greater improvement than this', Wise concluded, quoting also Aubrey and Lhuyd in Gibson's *Britannia*, and Henry Rowlands' *Mona Antiqua Restaurata* of 1723.

Arrived on White Horse Hill Wise 'was perswaded to look for the field of battle, and was greatly surprized to find my expectation answered in every respect'. The Iron Age hillfort of Uffington Castle ('a large Roman entrenchment') was occupied by the Danes, Hardwell Camp (a promontory fort to the west) 'fortified seemingly after the Saxon manner', defended king Ethelred's forces, Alfred's castle, an Iron Age fort to the south, had been declared Danish by Aubrey as quoted in the 1695 *Britannia*. The Horse itself, known from documents from the late twelfth century onwards, Wise thought a splendid work of art, 'enough to raise the admiration of every curious spectator, being designed in so masterlike a manner, that it may defy the painter's skill, to give a more exact description of that animal.' Asser had recorded that a Danish king and five counts were killed in the battle, and Wise identified the king's burial place in the megalithic chambered long barrow of Wayland's Smithy to the west of White Horse Hill. He quotes Aubrey (in Camden) to the effect that it was a mass of stones as if 'tumbled out of a cart', but here Gibson's editing had slipped up: in the *Monumenta* this is a quotation from Elias Ashmole, and Aubrey had in fact given a good plan and description of 'Wayland-Smyth'. Wise compared it with the Anglesey cromlechs illustrated by Rowlands and inevitably, for what he believed to be a Danish royal burial, with monuments in Ole Worm. He gives a not very good engraving of the site which, since Aubrey's much better plan remained unpublished, constitutes the earliest pictorial record of the barrow to be published. Wise then visited the tumulus–cemetery of the Lambourn Seven Barrows; here were the burial places of Asser's five Danish counts, and if the authority of the late medieval forgery of 'Ingulph's Chronicle' were allowed, the shady King Orguil and Count Fungus would bring the number up to seven, though as Wise recorded, the group included at least twenty, one a long barrow and some 'which Dr Stukely calls Celtick', or disc barrows. This is all good straightforward field observation, and he further collected the local folklore of Wayland's Smithy and Dragon Hill, and recorded the custom of 'scouring' the Horse.

Wise's apparently innocuous pamphlet provoked, in the next year, an unexpected and vitriolic attack with a long title opening, rather splendidly, *The Impertinence and Imposture of Modern Antiquaries Displayed . . . :* the author, 'Philalethes Rusticus', was probably a fellow-cleric, the Reverend William Asplin, Vicar of Banbury. Still in part entertaining, the squib would be forgotten if the author had not derided Wise's attribution of the Horse to the Saxons, and instead 'Might I therefore put in my Fancy among the rest, I should imagine that if the *Horse* were a *Standard* or *Banner*, it was a *British* one . . . and this Conjecture would be strengthened also by the *Figure* and *Posture* of the *Horse* in every circumstance; which are exactly the same with what we may observe upon some *British Coins* in *Speed.*' Now Aubrey, delightfully inconsistent, had at one point thought the Horse the standard of Hengist and Horsa and at another compared it with that on a British coin from Colchester, and Stukeley's daughter Anna was to write to him, after a visit to Berkshire in 1758, that it was 'very much in the scheme of the British horses on the reverse of their coins'. By the 1850s this stylistic comparison had been made afresh and independently by J.Y. Akerman, and became generally accepted by archaeologists. Recently a case has been made for a pagan Saxon origin, on the grounds that the present outline bears only a fortuitous resemblance to Iron Age artistic conventions owing to frequent recuttings over the years. If so, it is a surprising coincidence that the accidental end product should approximate so closely to a prehistoric prototype. It is worth noting that (as George North, supporting Wise against Philalethes in 1741 pointed out) the Speed coins published in 1611, and others later such as those in Gibson's Camden, show horses in a plump naturalistic Romanizing style, and not the disjointed beast as at Uffington or on the 'early inscribed' or Dobunic types largely ignored by the early antiquaries until Stukeley. Philalethes and probably Aubrey were doing no more than to point to alternative uses of horses as insignia, but Anna Stukeley could have known of more directly comparable coin types from her father's drawings.

Enter the Druids

The importance and widespread influence in eighteenth-century thought and emotion of an idealized and romanticized conception of the priests of the ancient Britons, the Druids, is the subject of a large literature to which the writer has contributed.[14] There is therefore no need here to do more than present the situation in brief outline, except so far as it contributes to our more limited objective of examining the ideas held about prehistoric Britain at this time.

The Renaissance rediscovered the Druids in the classical texts, particularly as these related to Gaul and Britain, but they had earlier engaged the attention of Hellenistic philosophers of the Alexandrian school, as well as the early Church Fathers, as representatives of barbarian philosophers with others like Indian gymnosophists, Persian magi, Egyptian sages and Hyperborean shamans. Clement of Alexandria claimed that Pythagorean doctrines were acquired from such sources, and in such a mood Druids easily became incorporated in the *prisca theologia*, the ancient wisdom of Hermes Trismegistus, as developed by the Hermetic Neoplatonists of the Italian fifteenth century and later in France and seventeenth-century England. The great Italian Neoplatonist, Giordano Bruno associated Druids with Hermes, as did Théodore Mayerne, physician to James I, in 1611; the Frenchman Guillaume Postel in 1551, and the Englishman, Edmund Dickenson in 1655, thought that the Druidic rites had been founded by Noah, thus giving the priesthood not only a high antiquity in world history, but a flavour of Christian respectability as well.

Little credit or attention was given to Hermes by the eighteenth century, and when Aylett Sammes described and illustrated the Druids in 1676 he depicts a barbarous scene enough; Camden gave the relevant classical texts and in 1695 Aubrey's tentative identification of stone circles as Druidic temples was in print with no hint of romantic overtones. The French had tended to cultivate heroic Druids as Gaulish law-givers, but Elias Schedius in his book *De Dis Germanis* of 1648 has a lively title-page of human sacrifices in an oak grove, in which a Druid with bloodstained knife is attended by a priestess slung round with a human skull, beating a drum with a pair of thigh-bones in a landscape strewn with corpses: no hint here of the wisdom of Hermes or the guidance of Noah.

After Aubrey's modest suggestion, the association of Druids with stone circles and megalithic monuments in Britain is usually, and with reason, attributed to the later writings of William Stukeley, but so far as publication is concerned, the presentation of Druids to the public was anticipated by two very different writers in 1723 and 1726, Henry Rowlands and John Toland. Of these, Toland, whom we met in the Introduction, is by far the more significant figure, even if the posthumous publication of his writings on Druids and stone circles was the later. Born in Ireland in 1670 and brought up a Londonderry Roman Catholic, he rapidly repudiated his religion, took a degree in the University of Edinburgh, and in 1696 shocked the churches by publishing his *Christianity Not Mysterious*, the first brilliantly able and controversial presentation of the case for Deism as an acceptable Christian faith. To go back to the doctrinal position of the Latitudinarian Church of England, the claim laid, especially by the Socinians, that 'because Christian revelation is from God and is therefore true, it must be rational and accessible',[15] could easily lead to the much more awkward conclusion of the Deists, forcibly put forward by Toland and soon by others, that the supernatural was irrelevant and unnecessary. John Locke presented the Latitudinarian case in his *Reasonableness of Christianity* in 1695, and it seems he had seen some version of Toland's book before its appearance in print in the following year and had written hastily in anticipation; public opinion at the time ranked them both as Socinians. The lack of historical sense that allowed the original, primitive, untutored savage to be presented as a rational being very like an educated eighteenth-century gentleman in comfortable circumstances was also to influence the idealization of the ancient Briton as a noble savage.

In 1694 Toland was in Oxford, where he met John Aubrey and Edmund Gibson, then editing the new *Britannia*. Gibson intended enlisting Toland's support for the Irish section, but soon found he could not stand his 'insolent conceited way of talking' and had no more to do with him. The Aubrey friendship was to have direct bearing on Toland's work on the Druids, which was to be summarized in three 'Letters' to the Irish peer, Robert first Viscount Molesworth, dated between June 1718 and April 1719 – 'Thus I have laid before your lordship a specimen of my *History of the Druids*'. Toland died in 1722, the book unwritten, but the *Letters* were published in 1726.[16] In the second, we have a little-known portrait of Aubrey in the last years of his life, as seen by an arrogant and abrasive young Irish intellectual of twenty-four

John Aubrey, Esq., a member of the royal society (with whom I became acquainted at Oxford, when I was a sojourner there) . . . was the only person I ever then met, who had a right notion of the temples of the Druids, or indeed any notion that the circles so often mentioned were such temples at all . . . he supply'd me with numerous instances of such monuments, which he was at great pains to observe and set down. And tho' he was extremely superstitious, or seem'd to be so: yet he was a very honest man and most accurate in his accounts of matters of fact. But the facts he knew, not the reflections he made, were what I wanted . . . Mr Aubrey show'd me several of Dr Garden's letters.

One can see Gibson's point; it seems likely that Aubrey had priority in attributing stone circles to the Druids, but Toland characteristically implies the reverse. He attributed all the standing stones ('obeliscs'), forts, duns and brochs of the Scottish Highlands to the Druids and then, 'I pass the certainty I have concerning *the temples of the Druids* . . . these temples are *circles of obeliscs* or erect stones . . . my Lord, I promise you no less than demonstration that those circles were Druids temples.' He goes on to instance those of Callanish, Stenness and Brodgar; Boscawen-un, Rollright, The Hurlers, Stonehenge and Avebury. He adds Welsh 'cromlechs' as altars from Lhuyd, and other megalithic monuments from France (La Pierre Levée at Poitiers) and the Channel Islands; his sources include the 1695 *Britannia*, James Wallace (1693) and John Brand's *Brief Description of Orkney* (1701) and particularly Martin Martin (1703) on the Western Isles. A fair showing for a literary hack, whose other numerous productions, from his Deist manifesto to his death in 1722, were polemic religious and political pamphlets.

His estimate of the Druids and their doctrines was characteristic. 'No heathen priesthood ever came up to the perfection of the Druidical', he wrote to Molesworth in his first Letter of 1718,

which was far more exquisite than any other such system: as having been much better calculated to beget ignorance, and an explicit disposition in the people, no less than to procure power and profit to the priests . . . To arrive at perfection in sophistry requires a long habit, as well as in juggling, in which last they were very expert: but to be masters of both, and withal to learn the art of managing the mob, which is vulgarly called *leading the people by the nose*, demands abundant study and exercise.

The attacks on 'priest-craft' recur obsessively, with all the bitterness of a spoiled Catholic: they cannot have endeared him to the Church, quite apart from the philosophy of his Deism.

Leaving the Deists for the moment, though we shall return to them when we come to the later Stukeley setting out to 'combat the deists from an unexpected quarter' in 1730, the *Mona Antiqua Restaurata* of the Reverend Henry Rowlands, published in 1723, was a second early presentation of Druids and megaliths to a British antiquarian audience. Rowlands was an Anglesey vicar and his book, in circulation in a manuscript form from about 1708, could not avoid the Druids recorded in the island by Tacitus. Rowlands owed much to Sammes and Bochart, believing Welsh to be really Hebrew, brought in by 'the first Planters of this Island',

being so near in descent, to the Fountains of true Religion and Worship, to have one of *Noah's* sons for Grandsire or Great-Grandsire, may be well imagin'd, to have carried and convey'd some of the Rites and Usages of that true Religion here, pure and untainted.

Here we go back to the Druidic rites of Noah's day as invented by Dickenson and Postel, and look forward to Stukeley introducing them to Britain 'soon after Noah's flood'. But Rowlands's view of British Druidic doctrines was no more complimentary than that of Toland. Once in Britain 'they soon after became ... abominably corrupted, and perverted into the grossest heathenish Fictions and Barbarities' propagated by 'insinuating priests' who obtained power 'and thereupon, to bear up a Port and Authority (no hard thing for them to do in that easy obsequious Age).'

In the 1723 manuscript draft Stukeley quotes Rowlands, together with Lhuyd's Camden additions on megalithic monuments. At the end, among some miscellaneous sources, he notes 'Mr Tolands history of the druids in Ld Molesworths hands'; later, in 1729, he wrote to a friend, 'Indeed I know my Lrd Molesworth'. Evidence suggests that in fact the unregenerate young Dr Stukeley, member of a notoriously free-thinking profession, knew Toland around 1718–19, and later in life, as a militantly anti-Deist churchman, conveniently forgot the acquaintanceship.

Stukeley as Archdruid

Although the 1723 text scarcely mentions Druids, there is no doubt that they bulked large in Stukeley's conversation. In the anti-medieval breakaway group of the Society of Roman Knights formed from the new Society of Antiquaries in 1722 by Stukeley, dissatisfied with the inertia of the parent body in field studies, he gave himself the name of Chyndonax, from an alleged inscription to a Druid published in 1623 from near Dijon. The nickname stuck and appears on the frontispiece of his Stonehenge volume of 1740. In 1723 he recorded at Avebury that 'Lord Winchelsea, Lord Hartford and the ladys came one day to visit the Druid as they called me'. There are no Druids in the appeal for subscriptions to a 'history of the ancient Celts' and on 'Celtic' religion contained in the preface to the 1724 *Itinerarium*, but by 1733, Sir John Clerk when visiting him found him writing a book 'on the Religion of the Druids and all their Temples and monuments', and the original title-page of the 1723 book was redrawn as *The History of the Religion and Temples of the Druids*. Stukeley had left London for Grantham in 1726 and three years later was ordained in the Church of England and secured the living of All Saints' Stamford. 'His friends think him crazy' said Thomas Hearne.

Stukeley's ordination, his enthusiastic acceptance into the Church by the Archbishop of Canterbury, and his subsequent essays in ecclesiastical controversy disguised as archaeology, will take us back to the Deists, but before that we should perhaps consider the hard facts of publishing in the 1720s. Then as now, a book would only be printed if financed privately, by subscription, by academic sponsorship by a University press, or as a commercial venture by the publisher, printer and bookseller. The decline in learning already commented on had rendered the ancient Britons and their monuments of little interest to the scholars, less to the wider reading public: they were no longer either a matter of academic prestige nor a business proposition. Subscription or personal funding in an unpopular cause alone remained. Stukeley's *Itinerarium* must have been printed by subscription, though no list survives or was printed for this folio volume of about 130,000 words and 100 engraved plates. Subscription lists were printed by Alexander Gordon in his *Itinerarium Septentrionale* in 1726 and by Henry Rowlands in *Mona Antiqua* in 1723: for the former (folio, 150,000 words, 66 plates) 272 names appear, for the latter (small quarto, 184,000 words, 10 plates) no less than 426 for the Dublin printing, mostly Welshmen. Francis Wise published his 28,000 word pamphlet privately in 1738 in an optimistic print run of 800 copies costing £25 to produce and selling at 1s 6d; with great difficulty he eventually disposed of 300 copies. In his preface to the *Itinerarium* dated 26 December 1724 Stukeley appealed for subscribers for a history of the Ancient Celts, 'four books in folio' of which two were to be on Stonehenge and Avebury respectively, with 'above 300 copper plates of a folio size, many of which are already engraven', but there can have been no adequate response, for publication of the two last folio volumes only, was not to be until 1740 (*Stonehenge*, 50,000 words, 35 plates) and 1743 (*Abury*, 75,000 words, 41 plates). The 1720s saw the publication of Rowlands (1723), Toland (1726), and a reprint of the three Jones–Charleton–Webb Stonehenge folios in 1725, and both the booksellers and the subscribing public may have felt they had had enough of Druids. And can it be coincidence that Stukeley's published volumes came out soon after his marriage to his second wife, Roger Gale's sister, who came with a marriage-portion of £10,000?

We must finally return to the religious controversy between the Church of England and the Deists with which the chapter opened and in which Stukeley entered with enthusiasm. Events followed one another rapidly after June 1739 when he wrote to his acquaintance William Wake, the scholarly Archbishop of Canterbury, announcing that his antiquarian studies of the Celts had led to his 'discovering some notions about the Doctrine of the Trinity which I think are not common' and offering himself for ordination in the Church. The Primate was enthusiastic at 'a time in which we wanted all the assistance we can get against the prevailing infidelity of the present wicked age', and Stukeley agreed 'with a resentment of that deluge of profaneness and infidelity', and was eager, as he put it later, 'to combat the deists from an unexpected quarter'. By 1730 he was the Reverend Dr Stukeley of All Saints' Stamford, composing the picture of the British Druids which was intended to further this cause. The Deists, as we saw, held that God had 'given mankind some rule or law for their conduct' from the time of the Creation, universal to all reasoning men at all times. Dr Matthew Tindall, no firebrand like Toland but a respectable Fellow of All Souls, expressed it in this same year, 1730, in his book-title *Christianity as old as the Creation, or the Gospel a republication of the Religion of Nature.*

Stukeley made his intention clear in the opening to his *Stonehenge* of 1740: it was to be the first of four volumes, not on prehistoric antiquities, but on 'Patriarchal Christianity or a Chronological History of the Origin and Progress of true Religion, and of Idolatry'. 'My intent is', he went on, 'to revive in the minds of the learned the spirit of Christianity . . . to warm our hearts into that true sense of Religion, which keeps the medium between ignorant superstition and learned free-thinking, between enthusiasm and the rational worship of God, which is no where upon earth done, in my judgement better than in the Church of *England*.' The Druids had come to Britain with 'an oriental colony . . . in the very earliest times, during the life of Abraham, or very soon after . . . soon after Noah's flood' under the leadership of the Tyrian Hercules, 'a worthy scholar of Abraham', and were 'of *Abraham's* religion intirely', and though 'we cannot say that Jehovah appeared personally to them' they had 'a knowledge of the plurality of persons in the Deity' with a religion 'so extremely like Christianity, that in effect it differ'd from it only in this; they believed in a Messiah who was to come into this world, as we believe in him that is come.' Combining Bochart, Sammes and Rowlands, and even some Hermetic Neoplatonism from Italian Renaissance sources, Patriarchal Christianity may seem to us not to differ much from a pious Deism, rather than an attack on that doctrine, and we would not be alone, for when in 1743 the *Abury* volume appeared, Stukeley's brother-in-law, Roger Gale, wrote to him, 'I little thought that Dr Tindall would have such a second to prove Christianity as old as the creation, though upon a different bottome and principles.' It was of no moment; the Deistic controversy raged between about 1720 and 1740, and then suddenly waned. No one was now interested in Patriarchal Christians or in stone circles, and the Druids moved out of archaeology and into the new world of noble savages and the fantasies of the romantic imagination.

The antiquarian sequel

There remained Stonehenge. By the 1720s the London to Bath road shifted its line to the south of Avebury, and the monument was again forgotten. But as the improvements in transport and the road system, leading to the development of the tourist trade, made Stonehenge, then as now, a required item on the itinerary of the curious, a spate of pamphlets on the monument appeared. They were all Druidic in approach and usually based on Stukeley, though the lectures given in Salisbury by a Mr Waltire in 1777 were more exotically original, for a contemporary records he 'endeavours to demonstrate Stonehenge has been immerged in the sea twelve miles deep, and that it was erected – judging by the precession of the equinoxes – at least seventeen thousand years ago'.[17]

But deep Druidic lore unexpectedly prompted the making of the first accurate and professional plan of the monument. The brilliantly talented John Wood, the architect of eighteenth-century Bath, seems from early youth to have conceived a passionate interest in a highly individual and eccentric Druidic past – 'I was long since led to conclude', he wrote in 1740, 'that the BRITISH DRUIDS, who flourished Ages before the birth of Christ, had not only PUBLIC EDIFICES . . . but such as were truly magnificent' Stonehenge 'appeared to me the Remains of a DRUIDICAL TEMPLE', and there is reason to think that the formal planning of the Circus at Bath, designed by Wood in 1725, was based on that of Stonehenge as given by Inigo Jones. Wood, as a young man in his early twenties, worked as a chief builder on the Cavendish–Harley estate in London, and must have formed a friendship with Edward Harley second Earl of Oxford (1689–1741), who in August 1740 visited Wood in Bath, where from 1725 he had been planning and executing the new building programme. Harley expressed interest in Wood's account of Stonehenge and Stanton Drew stone circles, and 'laid his Injunctions on me to make a correct Plan of them for his use', to 'comit my Thoughts concerning these Works . . . to Writing', and send him these, 'as well as copies of all the plans I shall make, that he might add the latter to his Book of Drawings of the like *British* Antiquities'.[18] By the end of September Wood was carrying out a professional architect's survey for three days at Stonehenge 'with proper Instruments and proper Assistants', including 'my Eldest son and chief Assistant . . . in this his first practical Lesson of Surveying' – John Wood the younger who was to continue the great architectural schemes in Bath. The account was written up and addressed to Harley as a 'Letter' on 15 December 1740, with fine measured plans. But Harley died in 1741 and Wood put the work aside until 1747, when it was published as *Choir Gawre, vulgarly called Stonehenge* . . . ; the title a sort of bogus Welsh for *Chorea Gigantum*. It is a very odd little book, expounding the most fantastically nonsensical Druidic inventions for which it is remembered today, but with a quarter of its 30,000 words devoted to a detailed account of the process of surveying, with engraved plans of an excellence not to be equalled before the end of the nineteenth century.[19]

A final mid-century statement of the antiquarian achievement of the day is provided by the Reverend William Borlase, a Cornish parson–naturalist who in 1754 published his *Antiquities historical and monumental of the County of Cornwall*. His setting, in the declining antiquarianism typified by his friend Francis Wise in Oxford, and the moribund Society of Antiquaries of London, has been sketched in Chapter I, but his book deserves more detailed comment here. The first impression on the reader today is its old-fashioned air. We are back to long opening disquisitions on 'the general Dispositions of Mankind in the first Ages after the Flood', with Welsh and Hebrew, Japhet and Gomer, Cimbri and Gauls; Bochart is much quoted as are Sammes, Stillingfleet's *Origines Sacrae* of 1662, Sheringham's *De Anglorum gentis origine* (1670), the Old Testament and the classical authors. These last two are again used at length in his long discussion of the Druids, as well as Schedius *De Dis Germanis* (1648), the more modern sources of Keysler's *Antiquitates selectae* . . . (1720), Toland, Rowlands, Martin Martin, Stukeley and the useful compendium of earlier sources, J.G. Frick, *Commentatio de Druidis* (1744). Apart from these, Borlase's book could have been written in the 1690s, and this fact serves to underline the stagnation of antiquarian studies from that time to his own. But he had, as we saw earlier, appreciated some sort of a technological sequence of stone, bronze and iron weapons.

Borlase thought that, 'that part of Noah's posterity which peopled Europe . . . the Cimbri or Celts as they were afterwards call'd' came to Gaul and thence to Britain, 'it being most probable that Britain had her first inhabitants from Gaul . . . The resemblance they preserv'd to the Eastern nations is very evident, as well from the Celtic language, being

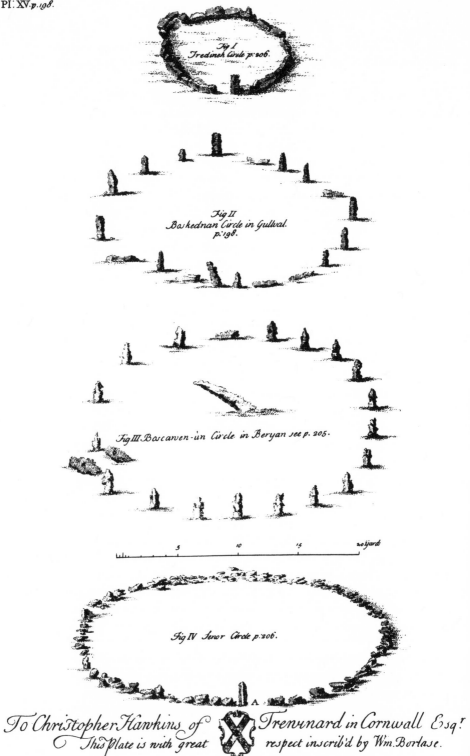

Fig I
Tredineh Circle p. 206.

Fig II
Boskednan Circle in Gullval.
p. 198.

Fig III. Boscawen-ùn Circle in Beryan see p. 205.

Fig IV Senor Circle p. 206.

To Christopher Hawkins of Trevinard in Cornwall Esq.
This plate is with great respect inscrib'd by Wm. Borlase.

16 Engravings of Cornish stone circles in William Borlase,
Antiquities . . . of the County of Cornwall (1754).

so much indebted to the Hebrew.' Phoenician tin traders came 'not till the year before Christ 450, but very likely sooner'. Greeks on the same quest in 160 BC. 'Of the British Religion' takes up sixteen long chapters in which the Druids are dealt with in detail, but not with admiration or respect – 'the barbarity, magic and grove-worship so justly laid to their charge . . . the frequency of their human sacrifices shocks us; their oak-worship looks singular and absurd.' Borlase has no doubt about them: they are not the gentlemanly philosophical clergy of Stukeley, but heathen idolaters worshipping stocks and stones, with reprehensible ancestors going back to Cain and the evil-doers of the Old Testament.

By Book III we come, in the good tradition of the early Royal Society, to an objective account of the various classes of Cornish antiquities. Rude Stone Monuments include standing stones, single or as Circular Monuments, denuded megalithic burial chambers ('Cromlehs' in Cornish) and, alas, many natural Rock Idols such as the Wring-cheese, Rocking Stones and eroded Rock Basins. All these are idols and 'among the most ancient British Monuments, the Stones-erect may justly claim a place' and 'can justly be ascribed to none but the Druids'. Plans or oblique views are given of such circles as the Boskednan Nine Maidens, Boscawen-Un and The Hurlers, but the stone setting of huts at Botallek are erroneously included, with some others. The megalithic tombs are not altars as Rowlands divined: 'it is very unlikely, if not impossible, that ever the Cromleh should have been an Altar for Sacrifice', for the top of the capstone 'was not easy to be got upon' in any ceremony, 'not to mention the horrid Rites' of the Druids (Stukeley had said the same in his 1723 manuscript). Instead, Borlase, noting the wide British and continental distribution of the type, felt 'it is very probable, therefore, that the use and intent' of such monuments 'was primarily to distinguish, and do honour to the dead, and also to inclose the dead body', and he gives plans and views of the Lanyon and Zennor chambers. Dealing with barrows and their burials he gives some of the earliest illustrations of prehistoric funerary pottery and a plan of a Scillonian passage-grave. He had clearly read Sir Thomas Browne's *Hydriotaphia*, which he quotes, for he gives a disquisition in elaborated prose on ancient burials, from Semiramis to Patroclus, and directly copies Browne in the phrase, 'Barrows therefore and Pyramids (solids the most simple next to barrows) bid fair to last as long as the world.' We have seen his sensible comments on the problem of prehistoric bronzes, and he also described and illustrated an important hoard from Carn Brea of ancient British coins, with a probable origin in Kent. Having very creditably dealt with prehistoric antiquities he goes on to cover the Roman and earlier medieval periods. As a workmanlike local survey in the tradition of Aubrey or Plot, it is all the more valuable for covering an important area of prehistoric Britain outside Wessex, within the boundaries of which so much of the earlier antiquarian effort had been concentrated.

From Borlase onwards Druids in various fantastic disguises persist through the eighteenth century to leave (in Collingwood's famous phrase on the ineptitude of provincial Roman art) an 'impression that constantly haunts the archaeologist, like a bad smell or a stickiness on the fingers'.[20] Increasingly they move away from any factual antiquarianism or archaeological evidence to the world of enjoyably bemused speculation, and, by way of Iolo Morganwg's first Gorsedd Circle on Primrose Hill in 1792 to shipwreck on William Blake's 'Albion's Ancient Druid Rocky Shore'. But in the meantime a very different climate of thought arose to offer, quite unconsciously, an impediment to the development of the practical archaeology that had emerged in the seventeenth, and was carried by Stukeley and Borlase into the eighteenth century.

Conjectural history

When we come to consider the antiquarian climate of opinion from the mid-eighteenth century we must remind ourselves of the Battle of the Ancients and Moderns touched on in Chapter 1. The Royal Society tradition of the empirical investigation of natural and artificial phenomena, that of the Moderns, came early under attack from the traditionalist men of letters, the Ancients. Already in 1694 William Wotton, in his *Reflections upon Ancient and Modern Learning* was saying 'The Humour of the Age, as to those things is visibly altered from what it was Twenty or Thirty years ago', and while the Royal Society had 'weathered the rude attacks' of its critics, 'yet the sly insinuations of the *Men of Wit*' had discredited science in the eyes of the educated public.[21] As Joseph Levine recently put it

The quarrel between the Ancients and the Moderns had laid the issue bare: What was the use of learning to a gentleman? For a man of the world, the object was a smattering of polite learning, a classical literary education that would furnish the necessary polish to shine in the fashionable circles of the great world. It was a matter of *style*.[22]

In France the quarrel was pursued with entrenched bitterness between the men of letters, *les philosophes*, and those of antiquarian learning, *les érudits*; the former, favoured by fashion and prophets of the

Enlightenment, included Diderot, d'Alembert, Voltaire and the circle of the *Encyclopédie*; among the antiquaries Diderot's arch-enemies were the Comte de Caylus and the other members of the *Académie des Inscriptions*. On his first visit to Paris in 1763 young Edward Gibbon, aged twenty-six and with his mind already set in the mould of a great historian, was indignantly contemptuous of the division: 'I could not approve the intolerant zeal of the philosophers and Encyclopaedists' – but he warmly acknowledged 'the good sense and learning of the principal members of the Academy of Inscriptions'. Already in the Salon of 1740 Jean Baptiste Chardin had exhibited a painting, 'Le Singe Antiquaire', in which an erudite ape sits in his fashionable day-gown, surrounded by his numismatic books and collections, peering at a coin with his lens. The ancient state of mankind was the proper study of the philosophers, untrammelled by the petty facts of the antiquary.[23]

Scotland, its intellectuals always closely in touch with France and with their own propensity for philosophical speculation, had by 1748, with the publication of Montesquieu's *Esprit des lois* found a congenial text by a French *philosophe*, with an Edinburgh edition by David Hume two years later. There then followed a series of essays in what Professor Dugald Stewart, writing retrospectively of Adam Smith in 1794, said, 'I shall take the liberty of giving the title of *Theoretic or Conjectural History*', concerning itself with the evolution of human society from its earliest beginnings and from the pens of political economists and speculative philosophers such as Adam Smith, Adam Fergusson, Lord Kaimes and Lord Monboddo from the 1760s to the 1790s. 'On most of these subjects', Stewart went on, 'very little information is to be expected from history', since 'many of the most important steps' in social development took place before any documentary record, so that 'in this want of direct evidence, we are under the necessity of supplying the place of fact by conjecture.' This the philosphers had no hesitation in doing, and from Montesquieu, Rousseau (*Discours sur l'inégalité* 1755) and Condorcet in France, to Adam Fergusson (*Essay on the History of Civil Society*, 1767), Adam Smith (*Sketches of the History of Man*, 1774), Lord Monboddo (*Origin and Progress of Language*, 1773–92) and James Beattie (*Elements of Moral Science*, 1790–93) in Scotland, a consistent hypothetical sequence was put forward. 'The gradual progress of man', observed Adam Smith, follows a four-fold scheme 'beginning with hunting and fishing, advancing to flocks and herds, and then to agriculture and commerce', and this with minor elaborations (Monboddo boldly started with man as a speechless quadruped) was generally accepted as answering all the necessary questions. With 'primitive' men taken uncritically from travellers' tales, pasturage from the Old Testament patriarchs, agriculture from founder-myths such as that of Triptolemus and the rest from early legend and history, *les philosophes* by-passed *les érudits* by ignoring them, and wrote prehistory without benefit of archaeology. As to chronology, the Conjectural Historians assume, without saying so, that their starting-point is the post-diluvial peopling of the Old and New Worlds; Rousseau, a muddle-headed romantic and no scholar, seems to have envisaged a vast but vague time scale. For the rest, the Grand Scheme was superior to precise chronology and hard facts, the province of the sedulous ape looking at antiquity through his myopic quizzing-glass.[24]

The Scottish philosophers had in fact little they could have turned to for the prehistoric past beyond Sibbald and elf-bolts, and they were hardly likely to have considered the Wiltshire downs or the Cornish moors. English antiquaries ignored such things. Thomas Pownall, a remarkable man with first-hand knowledge of American Indians as successively Lieutenant-Governor of New Jersey and Governor of Massachusetts between 1755 and 1760, read a paper on Newgrange to the Society of Antiquaries of London in 1770 in which he put up a very interesting scheme of '*Woodland-men*, living on the fruits, fish and game of the forest' to whom 'the Land-worker succeeded. He *settled* on the land, became a fixed inhabitant, and increased and multiplied'. In Europe the first were 'Cumbri, Umbri, Velgi, Bolgae or Belgae' and so Celts; the latter Phoenicians with their missionary Druids: Sammes and Stukeley sadly in the ascendant. The paper, printed in *Archaeologia* three years later, seems to have provoked no comment. The ancient Briton remained substantially where he was nearly a century before.[25]

'Facts, not Theory'

In the antiquarian pursuit of the prehistoric past little progress was made from the state of knowledge summarized in the 1695 *Britannia* until the beginning of the nineteenth century. Stukeley's individual contribution was his fieldwork and record, unprecedented in its detail and quality, at Avebury and Stonehenge, but otherwise he did not advance on Aubrey or Lhuyd. Further development in the understanding of archaeological evidence was impeded by two factors: failure to achieve a classification of the available artifacts in the field or museum, and the lack of any technique for obtaining new primary evidence by controlled excavation. Even in the doldrums of the field sciences after the 1720s considerable progress was made in classification and taxonomy by the natural historians studying plants, birds, butterflies and so on, but here the subject-matter was essentially different from that of archaeology, for it was profuse, inexhaustible and attractive. Gardening and bird-watching gratified romantic sentiments as well as contributing to taxonomic knowledge, and the natural world was not one of rare, unique and unattractive objects, but of continuously self-renewing and often beautiful species, very different from the occasional flint arrowhead or bronze axe. Nor were artifacts collected or recorded in sufficient numbers to make quantitative classification possible. It was not until the late nineteenth century that the activities of collectors following the soil disturbance arising from the exploitative activities of the Industrial Revolution – quarries, canals, railways – that the basic classification of prehistoric artifacts could take place: that of stone implements in 1872 and of bronzes in 1881 by Sir John Evans, of pottery and other grave-finds by John Thurnam in 1869–73, the latter made possible by barrow-digging activity since 1800.[26]

This brings us to our second impediment to the investigation of prehistoric Britain, the fundamental lack, until the close of the nineteenth century, of adequate excavation technique which, with an understanding of the artifacts and their stratification, could enable archaeological evidence to be recovered under controlled conditions.

As we saw in Chapter 4, apart from medieval and later treasure-hunting,[27] the digging into barrows for information goes back to the earlier seventeenth century when Sir John Oglander 'digged for my experience in soome of the moore awtientist', and by mid-century Sir Thomas Browne suggesting 'subterraneous enquiry by cutting through one of them either directly or cross-wise', or by the 1720s Stukeley digging trenches across barrows near Stonehenge at the instance of Lord Pembroke. And then, in 1800, there suddenly began a campaign of digging into both long and round barrows in Wiltshire, resulting over a decade in the excavation of over three hundred and fifty,[28] when the publication of the resultant mass of new primary archaeological material by the sponsor of the enterprise, Sir Richard Colt Hoare, in two noble folio volumes, was prefaced by an introduction opening with the proud boast "WE SPEAK FROM FACTS, NOT THEORY". Such is the motto I adopt, and to this text I shall most strictly adhere. I shall not seek among the fanciful regions of romance an origin for our Wiltshire Britons.' The achievement of the excavator, William Cunnington, and his patron Colt Hoare, forms an appropriate landmark, exactly at the end of the eighteenth century, to close our survey of earlier antiquarian achievement, for it marks the end of one tradition, going back to Camden, and forms its last expression. It also heralds a break from one approach to the prehistoric past, that of the antiquaries, to a new one, that of the archaeologists allying themselves for the first time since the Restoration with the sciences as they joined with the geologists to determine the antiquity of man.[29]

The stimulus for all this Wiltshire barrow-digging is still rather obscure. William Cunnington, a respectable but not outstanding wool merchant of Heytesbury, appears to have suffered from severe headaches probably caused by mild acromegaly, and, in his own words, 'Doctors Fothergill and Beddoes told me I must ride out or die'. Like Stukeley with the gout, he took to riding over the downs for his health, developed an untutored taste for antiquities, and in 1800 suddenly dug into a small barrow and recovered a cremated burial in a pot with a small bronze knife. One of the friends with him at the time was the MP for Wilts, H.P. Wyndham, with a desultory interest in writing the history of the county: he then asked Cunnington to dig into a long barrow near Heytesbury, to prove his belief that it was a battle-barrow (we are back to Dugdale) and not that of an Archdruid as Stukeley thought. They could, of course, not understand what they found in a limited hole made by an unsupervised labourer, and Wyndham, now with his friend the Reverend William Coxe, rector of Bemerton and later Archdeacon of Salisbury, and of antiquarian tastes, put Cunnington to dig into no less than four more long barrows, some huge, apparently in all cases with one labourer. The antiquaries were satisfied that they had indeed evidence that the mounds were 'certainly battle-barrows' with 'marks of carnage' and sometimes 'officers of distinction' or 'a man of very superior rank' with an iron sword. These were of course Saxon secondary burials. Cunnington, now keeping his own notes, remained unconvinced. Round barrows were now being dug, but Wyndham and Coxe had lost interest by 1803, and the project of a History of Wiltshire was taken on, and brought to a triumphal conclusion, by Sir Richard Colt Hoare of Stourhead. With the project he took on the patronage of Cunnington, who was to become a personal friend and responsible for providing the basic archaeology of the prehistoric prelude to the Wiltshire history, the patrician volumes of *Ancient Wiltshire* (1812–19), opening with the arresting words we have just quoted.

Sir Richard Colt Hoare was a wealthy country gentleman, a member of the banking family who in 1785 succeeded as second

Baronet with the great estate of Stourhead in Wiltshire, so superbly landscaped by his grandfather Henry in the 1740s. Well read and widely travelled, of great taste, sensibility and charm, he was early attracted to antiquarian pursuits, and with quiet competence and skill in organization set on foot an enterprise that deserves the distinction of being the first piece of archaeological field research in this country planned as a co-operative undertaking. Hoare, as instigator, planner and paymaster, first enlisted Cunnington as excavation director in the field with two diggers he had trained in at least rudimentary technique, Stephen and John Parker. He then, as draughtsman–surveyor, had Philip Crocker seconded from the newly established Ordnance Survey (and later took him on as steward at Stourhead). For consultants, he turned, not always wisely, to Wyndham, Coxe and the Reverend Thomas Leman, a pompous and opinionated cleric–antiquary who pontificated darkly from Bath. Hoare's aim was unprecedented and admirable, and to the work of the team was due a sudden access of primary evidence, on a scale hitherto unthought of, deliberately sought as a means to knowledge and recorded with, though it seems pitifully inadequate today, detail at a new standard. Not only were the grave-groups from the barrows described and preserved as units rather than as disparate curiosities, but Crocker as surveyor produced new plans of hillforts and settlement sites for the first time. Archaeologists have used the record of *Ancient Wiltshire* up to the present day and all credit goes to Hoare, Cunnington and the rest of the team, but when we turn to the work in the context of eighteenth-century antiquarian knowledge, we see at once how lamentably inadequate were the standards of technique and scholarship within which the work was necessarily carried out. Sir Richard's facts were obtained by means that were hardly better than medieval, and the Theories he abjured but which conditioned his understanding were those of a century earlier.

The evidence is best assembled from Cunnington's letters and the excavation journals that formed the basis of the published accounts edited by Hoare. Excavation normally took the form of digging a hole from the top of the mound by workmen with pick and shovel, not necessarily under supervision. Even when Cunnington was present he could record

It is much to be regretted that this little vessel of such superior taste, which was found whole, should have been beaten to pieces by the pick-axe, and what occasioned me greater vexation, I saw the pick-axe go into it before I could cry out to the man to stop.

An unfortunate mistake, but nothing more. Hoare's contribution to technique was to design a special blunt knife,[30] the precursor of the mason's pointing trowel adopted by modern excavators (though also used by Cunnington's men): 'mind that the men bring both their knives with them', wrote Hoare to Cunnington in 1805. No plans, drawings or sections were ever thought necessary as records. The process was known as 'opening' – 'I have never known the barrows open so well' said Cunnington in the next year, and the phrase was to be much used in the nineteenth century. Opening soon became popular in Wiltshire, for in 1812 the young antiquarian draughtsman Charles Stothard wrote from Salisbury

I have found a young antiquary, who, from practice, can open a barrow as nicely as you could cut up an apple pye; and from his description, it is done much after the same manner[31]

and so it would be for a century to come.

Crocker's plans of earthworks were something new, but they hardly served knowledge, as they were surveyed unintelligently by someone who, however conscientious, had no understanding of what he was recording. It was hardly his fault: no one else had, any more than in Leland's or Camden's day. His drawings of the grave-goods from the barrows met, in Gombrich's terms, the 'purpose and requirements of the society in which the given language gains currency' but these fall far short of the requirements of archaeologists today.[32] In all, from the viewpoint of technique, *Ancient Wiltshire* shows no advance over the late seventeenth century.

The model of the prehistoric past within which the Hoare group operated derived largely from the ideas of the old-fashioned Thomas Leman, to whom the written testimony of the classical writers was still all-important: he was an Ancient, not a Modern. He did, however, in a letter to Cunnington, sketch out a stone–bronze–iron sequence

I think we distinguish three great eras in the arms of offence found in our barrows 1st those of bone and stone, certainly belonging to the primeval inhabitants in the savage state, and which may be safely attributed to the Celts. 2nd those of brass, probably imported into this island from the more polished nations of Africa in exchange for our tin, and which may be given to the Belgae. 3rd those of iron, introduced but a little before the invasions of the Romans

This is substantially where William Borlase had arrived in 1754: the polished Africans were of course Phoenicians. As to the date of the round barrows, Cunnington ventured that they might be 'from five hundred to a thousand years before Caesar's invasion'; the Hoare circle misguidedly accepted as authentic the forged 'Richard of Cirencester' account of Roman Britain sponsored by Stukeley, which dated the arrival of the Belgae in Britain at 350 BC. And Hoare saw the Wiltshire barrow-builders in the most unflattering light of pessimistic primitivism. 'Perhaps a more just, spirited and appropriate account could not have been given of our primitive Britons', he wrote, than that given by Tacitus in Book 46 of the *Germania* of the last and most benighted northern tribe he describes, the Fenni. Hoare quoted him in Latin and in English translation, beginning, 'Nothing can equal the ferocity of the Fenni, nor is there anything so disgusting as their filth and poverty . . . '. The hillforts surveyed by Crocker were still, as they were in Aubrey's day, Saxon or Danish when not Roman, though Cunnington was privately 'for ascribing such works . . . to the Britons, and would call them British towns'. This was a step forward, and so was his recognition of 'little squares formed by lynchets (the mark of ancient agriculture) all over the sides of our hills'. From Roman finds in these field boundaries 'I think the evidence is full proof that this ancient agriculture was the work of the Romanized Britons'. Like Stukeley observing the same field systems, he saw untutored Britons ignorant of agriculture until civilized by Rome.

We reach the end of the eighteenth century, and of our survey of the pursuit of the ancient Briton, at a true turning-point, and not one set by the conventional centennial division of time. *Ancient Wiltshire* of 1812–19, recording the work of the previous decade, encapsulates the state of knowledge of prehistoric Britain reached, after unprecedented effort in the field, by the antiquaries of the day, and as we analyze it, we see that it constitutes little advance over the views of Borlase in the 1750s, or indeed those of Stukeley in the 1720s. The model of the prehistoric past as presented at the end of the seventeenth century was in fact, with only minor improvements, that of the nineteenth century. In conclusion it is permissible to overstep the boundary of the years and see the extraordinary result of Cunnington's and Hoare's work, in a brief postscript.

Aftermath

Inspired by the novel results of the Wiltshire campaign, barrow-digging swiftly moved into fashion and then into antiquarian passion, a Victorian phenomenon like the Great Fern Craze in natural history from 1837. With excavation techniques rarely superior to and frequently of a standard below that of Cunnington, country gentlemen, parsons and doctors took the field and attacked barrows and cairns from Dorset to Yorkshire, from Cornwall to Derbyshire. Marsden has estimated a convervative figure of over 2,500 such barrow openings during the century,[33] and the records (when published) make melancholy reading. A huge number of antiquities, almost wholly of Bronze Age date, was found in contexts inadequately or unintelligently recorded, and while a high proportion survived to form the nucleus of the collections of museums today, much was lost over the years. Faced with this access of new evidence, the barrow-diggers were defeated, their concept of the prehistoric past feeble and bewildered and still that of the eighteenth century. In 1866 Charles Warne, in his *Celtic Tumuli of Dorset*, was in despair:

Who were the Ancient Britons, and by what races were the tumuli of Dorset and Britain . . . are even now far from being satisfactorily determined . . . the obscurity which now on every side surrounds all things connected with the era in which they lived, is almost, if not wholly impenetrable.

It was no better a decade later in Yorkshire. Canon William Greenwell, who personally dug 297 barrows, summed up his conclusion in *British Barrows* (1877):

One thing is certain, that they are the burial mounds of a people who occupied the Wolds antecedent to the conquest of Britain by the Romans . . . and we need not fear that we are attributing too high an antiquity to them, if we say they belong to a period which centres more or less on 500 BC.

The technique of excavation was to remain at the primitive level of the seventeenth and eighteenth centuries until it was revolutionized and set on a recognizably modern footing by General Pitt-Rivers in 1880–1900.

The year 1800, by a curious coincidence, does make a point of departure of British prehistory into its momentous new phase, the establishment of the high antiquity of man and his artifacts, in conjunction with the newly maturing science of geology, in 1859. In 1797 John Frere had found at Hoxne in Suffolk flint implements with bones of extinct animals: 'the situation in which these weapons were found may tempt us to refer them to a very remote period indeed, even beyond that of the present world'. His report was published in *Archaeologia* for 1800, and was to be recalled by the geologist Joseph Prestwich when, with the archaeologist John Evans, he made his famous visit to the Somme gravels in 1859 which demonstrated without doubt the contemporaneity of stone implements with an extinct Pleistocene fauna.[34] The same year Charles Darwin published his *Origin of Species*, and the concept of the ancient Briton, hardly altered since it was formed at the beginning of the eighteenth century, suddenly became archaeological rather than antiquarian, Modern rather than Ancient.

But the antiquity of man was to receive opposition from a source long since forgotten as in any way an opponent, the Church of England. From the days when eminent churchmen of the Restoration, such as the Reverend Joseph Glanvill or the Bishop of Rochester, Thomas Sprat, had enthusiastically championed the New Science, clerical concern for the study of ancient man was benevolent and encouraging when not indifferent. But the Victorian Evangelical church, apprehensive of something on which it was ill-informed, thought otherwise. It was Blomfield, Bishop of London 1828–56, who banned ladies from attendance at the geology lectures in King's College lest they should be corrupted by the dangerous subject; Lord Shaftesbury (1801–85) who wrote of the Bible, 'The blessed old book is "God's Word Written" from the very first syllable down to the last'; *The Impregnable Rock of Holy Scripture* was written in 1890 by Mr Gladstone.

PENICUIK LIBRARY.

17 Retrospective antiquarianism. Bookplate of Clerk of Penicuik, early nineteenth century, with supporters added to the original arms in 1807. These are, dexter 'a naked savage, wreathed about the middle with oak leaves', with bow and arrow and 'the skin of a wild beast hanging behind his back'; sinister, a Druid priest. The Ancient Briton (or Caledonian) and Druid look back to the antiquarian interests of Sir John Clerk, second Baronet (1684–1755), friend of Stukeley and the leading Scottish antiquary of his day.

Notes

INTRODUCTION [pp 1–12]

1 For the potentialities here, cf. T.H. Cocke, 'Rediscovery of the Romanesque' in *English Romanesque Art 1066–1200*, Arts Council Exhib. Catalogue, London 1984, 360–66.

2 M.J.S. Rudwick, *The Meaning of Fossils*, London 1972, Preface.

3 *Times Lit. Supp.* June 3–9, 1988, 603.

4 P. Medawar, *The Art of the Soluble*, London 1967, 79.

5 G. Daniel, *The Origins and Growth of Archaeology*, Harmondsworth 1967, 133–141 with quotations.

6 J.M. Crook, *The British Museum*, Harmondsworth 1973, 127.

CHAPTER 1 [pp 13–35]

1 See particularly R. Weiss, *The Renaissance Discovery of Classical Antiquity*, Oxford 1969; A. Momigliano, 'Ancient History and the Antiquarian', *Studies in Historiography*, London 1966, 1–39.

2 General studies include Basil Willey, *The Seventeenth-Century Background*, Cambridge 1934; *The Eighteenth-Century Background*, London 1940; David Douglas, *English Scholars*, London 1939; T.D. Kendrick, *British Antiquity*, London 1950; Stuart Piggott, *Ruins in a Landscape*, Edinburgh 1976; J.M. Levine, *Dr Woodward's Shield*, Univ. California Press 1977; *Humanism and History*, Cornell Univ. Press 1987; I.G. Brown, *The Hobby-Horsical Antiquary*, Nat. Library Scotland, 1980. Individual biographical studies are quoted below.

3 J.M. Levine, *Dr Woodward's Shield*, is a full study of Woodward and his times.

4 Joan Evans, *A History of the Society of Antiquaries*, Oxford 1956, 167–8.

5 There is no full-length study of Camden, but see Kendrick, *British Antiquity*, Chap. VIII; Piggott, *Ruins* no. III; H. Trevor-Roper, *Renaissance Essays*, London 1985, no.8. In the quotations from *Britannia* the 1695 English translation of the original Latin is used throughout.

6 A. Agarde, 'Of the Diversity of Names of this Island', in T. Hearne (ed.) *A Collection of Curious Discourses*, Oxford 1720, 160. This is a collection of essays read to the Society; Joan Evans, *Hist. Soc. Antiq.*, 8–15.

7 Aylett Sammes, *Britannia Antiqua Illustrata*, London 1676, 38.

8 John Aubrey, *Memoires of Naturall Remarques in the County of Wilts*, 1685; ed. John Britton 1847, repr. 1969, Preface.

9 Anthony Wood, *Life and Times* s. ann. 1656, Llewelyn Powis ed. Oxford 1961, 73.

10 For Hearne, Douglas, *English Scholars*, 226–48; S. Piggott, 'Antiquarian Studies', in L.S. Sutherland & L.G. Mitchell, *Hist. Univ. Oxford: The Eighteenth Century*, Oxford 1986, 757–77.

11 Hugh Trevor-Roper, *Renaissance Essays*, 137.

12 M. Maclagan, 'Genealogy and Heraldry in the Sixteenth and Seventeenth Centuries', in L. Fox (ed.) *English Historical Scholarship in the Sixteenth and Seventeenth Centuries*, Oxford 1956, 31.

13 Sir William Temple, *Introduction to*

the History of England, 1695, quoted by J.M. Levine, *Humanism and History*, 166.

14 R.G. Collingwood, *The Idea of History*, Oxford 1946, 12; cf. Piggott, *Ruins*, 2.

15 Best summaries for our purpose, C. Webster, *The Great Instauration*, London 1975; ibid. (ed.) *The Intellectual Revolution of the Seventeenth Century*, London 1974; M. Hunter, *Science and Society in Restoration England*, Cambridge 1981.

16 O. Impey & A. Macgregor (eds), *The Origins of Museums*, Oxford 1985; A. Macgregor, *Tradescant's Rarities: Essays on the Foundation of the Ashmolean Museum 1683*, Oxford 1983; R.F. Ovenell, *The Ashmolean Museum 1683–1894*, Oxford 1986.

17 T. Sprat, *History of the Royal Society*, 1667, 436, quoted by Joan Evans, *Hist. Soc. Antiqs.*, 29.

18 M.J.G. Rudwick, *The Meaning of Fossils*, London & New York 1972, 74; P. Rossi, *The Dark Abyss of Time*, Chicago & London 1984, 16.

19 R. Plot, *Natural History of Staffordshire*, Oxford 1686, 392.

20 R. Plot, *Natural History of Oxfordshire*, Oxford 1677, 315.

21 For Aubrey, Anthony Powell, *John Aubrey and his Friends*, London 1948; Michael Hunter, *John Aubrey and the Realm of Learning*, London 1975; Stukeley, Stuart Piggott, *William Stukeley: an Eighteenth Century Antiquary*, London & New York 1985; Borlase, P.A.S. Pool, *William Borlase*, Truro 1986; Wise, S. Piggott in *Hist. Univ. Oxford: XVIII Cent.*, 757–77; Sibbald, S. Piggott, *Ruins*, 135–39.

22 There is no full study of Plot. *Dict. Nat. Biog.*; R.T. Gunther *Early Science in Oxford* III & IV, Oxford 1925; Ovenell, *Ashmolean Museum*, 31–63; his proposal to Dr Fell was printed by T. Hearne, *Itinerary of John Leland*, Oxford 1710–12, II, 165–74; S. Piggott, *Antiq.* LIX, 1985, 206–09.

23 Lhuyd still awaits a biographer. R.T. Gunther, *Life and Letters of Edward Lhwyd* (Early Science in Oxford XIV), Oxford 1945; F. Emery, *Edward Lhuyd FRS*, Cardiff 1971; J.L. Campbell & J.D. Thomson, *Edward Lhuyd in the Scottish Highlands*, Oxford 1963; Gwyn Walters, 'Introduction' to *Camden's Wales ... by Edward Lhuyd ... Carmarthen* 1984.

24 David Douglas, *English Scholars*, 68; Kendrick, *British Antiquity*, 76, 133.

25 For the questionnaires, cf. S. Piggott, *William Stukeley*, 21.

26 M. Hunter, *Antiq.* LXV, 1971, 113–21; 187–92.

27 William Wooton, *Reflections upon Ancient and Modern Learning*, 1694, quoted by R.F. Jones *et al.* (eds) *The Seventeenth Century* Stanford Univ. Press 1951, 41–74; M. 'Espinasse in Webster (ed.) *Intellectual Revolution*, 349.

28 John Locke, *Essay concerning Human Understanding*, 1690, quoted by Willey, *Seventeenth Century* Chap XI; Joseph Addison, *Tatler* 216, 1710, quoted by 'Espinasse, *Intellectual Revolution*, 354.

29 D.E. Allen, *The Naturalist in Britain*, London 1976, 10–11.

30 Joan Evans, *Hist. Soc. Antiqs.*

31 J.G. Jenkins, *The Dragon of Whaddon*, High Wycombe 1953.

32 S. Piggott, *Antiq.* LX, 1986, 115–22.

33 Quoted by Roy Porter, *The Making of Geology*, Cambridge 1977, 66.

34 Quoted by J.M. Levine, *Dr Woodward's Shield*, 67.

CHAPTER 2 [pp. 36–53]

1 Quoted, for instance, by Glyn Daniel, *The Three Ages*, Cambridge 1943, 7, from Boswell's *Life of Johnson*, Wednesday 29 April 1778.

2 William Whewell, *History of the Inductive Sciences*, 1837, quoted by C.C. Gillispie, *Genesis and Geology*, Harper Torchbook ed. 1959, 140.

3 J.J. Dortous de Mairan, quoted by P. Rossi, *The Dark Abyss of Time*, Chicago & London 1984, 144.

4 Keith Thomas, *Religion and the De-*

cline of Magic, London 1971, Peregrine ed. 1982, 172.

5 H. Trevor-Roper, *Catholics, Anglicans and Puritans*, London 1987, 120–65 (Ussher); P. Rossi, *Dark Abyss of Time*, 144 (Vossius); G.L. Davies, *The Earth in Decay*, London n.d. but 1969, 13–14 (Ussher and Lloyd); S. Toulmin & J. Goodfield, *The Discovery of Time* 1965, Harmondsworth 1967, 71–73; N. Cohn, *The Pursuit of the Millennium*, 1957, Paladin (London) 1970, 108–110 (Joachim of Fiore).

6 H.F. Kearney in Webster (ed.) *Intellectual Revolution*, 226; S. Piggott, *Antiq.* LX, 1986, 115–22.

7 The literature of the Hermetic traditions is enormous; in general Frances Yates, *Giordano Bruno and the Hermetic Tradition*, London & Chicago 1964, pbk. 1978; Keith Thomas, *Religion & the Decline of Magic*, 267–70; S. Piggott, *Antiq.* LX, 1986, 115–22 (Stukeley).

8 Biblical commentaries are legion; cf. here A. Jones *et al.* (eds) *The Jerusalem Bible*, London & New York 1966, 7–12; S. Cook, *An Introduction to the Bible*, Harmondsworth 1945; J.B. Pritchard, *Ancient Near Eastern Texts relating to the Old Testament*, 2nd.ed. Princeton 1955; R.C. Dentan (ed.) *The Idea of History in the Ancient Near East*, Yale Univ. Press 1955; D. Diringer, *Writing*, London & New York 1962, 123.

9 Cf. the absurdly short chronology of S. Piggott, *Neolithic Cultures of the British Isles*, Cambridge 1954.

10 Keith Thomas, *Man and the Natural World*, London 1983.

11 For the concept of anachronism cf. Keith Thomas, *Religion & the Decline of Magic*, 509; coach in Lynn White, *Medieval Religion and Technology*, Univ. of California 1978, 205.

12 A pioneer work was F.E. Zeuner, *A History of Domesticated Animals*, London 1963; see also J. Clutton-Brock, *Domesticated Animals*, London 1981; I.L. Mason (ed) *Evolution of Domesticated Animals* London & New York 1984; P.J. Ucko & G.W. Dimbleby (eds),

The Domestication and Exploitation of Plants and Animals, London 1969; S.J.M. Davis, *The Archaeology of Animals*, London 1988.

13 A. Golding, *The rare and singular worke of Pomponius Mela . . .* 1590, quoted by M.T. Hodgen, *Early Anthropology in the Sixteenth and Seventeenth Centuries*, Philadelphia 1964, 40.

14 R.H. Popkin, *Isaac La Peyrère*, Leiden & New York 1987; D.C. Allen, *The Legend of Noah*, Urbana 1949, 133; P. Rossi, *Dark Abyss*, 132 ff.

15 E. Iversen, *The Myth of Egypt and its Hieroglyphs*, Copenhagen 1961; J.D. Wortham, *British Egyptology 1549–1906*, Newton Abbot 1971; M. Pope, *The Story of Decipherment*, London & New York 1975.

16 Denys Hay, *Polydore Vergil*, Oxford 1952, 52–78; J.M. Levine, *Dr Woodward's Shield*, Univ. California Press 1977, 70, 75.

17 S. Piggott, *Antiq* XII, 1938, 323; R. Bernheimer, *Wild Men in the Middle Ages*, Cambridge, Mass. 1952; E. Dudley & M.E. Novak (eds) *The Wild Man Within*, Univ. Pittsburg 1972.

18 S. Piggott, *Ruins*, 5.

19 M. Marples, *White Horses and other Hill Figures*, London 1949, 204–12.

20 T.D. Kendrick, *British Antiquity*, 69–73; 105–06.

21 Monboddo is quoted at length and ridiculed by T.L. Peacock in his novel *Melincourt* ((1817); he had taken up the theme earlier in *Headlong Hall* (1816), with Mr Cranium).

22 S. Piggott, *William Stukeley*, 22.

23 J. Douglas ('Tumboracus') in *Gents. Mag.* 1789, quoted by R. Jessup, *Man of Many Talents*, London 1975, 117.

24 Keith Thomas, *Man in the Natural World*, 168.

25 J. Frere, letter of 1797 published in *Arch.* XII, 1800, 204; G. Daniel, *Origins and Growth of Archaeology*, Harmondsworth 1967, 57–59.

26 Quoted by P. Rossi, *Dark Abyss*, 73; for Rousseau, cf. ibid 264.

CHAPTER 3 [pp. 54–86]

1 D.C. Allen, *The Legend of Noah*, Urbana 1949; J. Godwin, *Athanasius Kircher*, London & New York 1979 (good illustrations but dubious text).
2 J.G. Frazer, *The Golden Bough*, Abridged ed. 1929, 244.
3 *Paradise Lost*, VII, 980–85.
4 P. Rossi, *Dark Abyss of Time*, 152 ff.; F.Yates, *The Art of Memory*, London 1966 (Harmondsworth 1969, 221).
5 *Journ. Anthrop. Inst.* I, 1871, 363. I am grateful to Dr Andrew Sherratt for this surprising reference.
6 G.L. Davies, *Earth in Decay*, 38.
7 W. Raleigh, *History of the World*, 1614, I.VIII.ii; D.B. Quinn, *Ralegh and the British Empire*, Harmondsworth 1973, 141.
8 Quoted by G.L. Davies, *Earth in Decay*, 38.
9 R. Plot, *Natural History of Oxfordshire*, 113; M. Rudwick, *The Meaning of Fossils*, 37.
10 D.C. Allen, *Legend of Noah*, 86.
11 R. Verstegen, *Restitution...*, 105; fossils 113; wolves 120. Keith Thomas, *Man and the Natural World*, 273; J. Ritchie, *Influence of Man on Animal Life in Scotland*, Cambridge 1920, 115–21; C. Matheson, *Changes in the Fauna of Wales within Historic Times*, Cardiff 1932, 29–33; F. Zeuner, *Hist. Dom. Animals*, 82.
12 D.C. Allen, *Legend of Noah*, 130.
13 J.K. Wright, *Geographical Lore at the time of the Crusades*, Dover Books 1965, 233–5.
14 T. Browne, *Pseudodoxia Epidemica...* London 1646, Bk.VI, Ch.vi.
15 S. Piggott, *Ruins*, 55–75; D.C. Allen, *Legend of Noah*, 114.
16 T.D. Kendrick, *British Antiquity*, 65–77; D. Hay, *Polydore Vergil*, 157–61; S. Piggott, *Ruins*, 57–60; E. Iversen, *The Myth of Egypt*, 62.
17 D.B. Quinn, *Ralegh and the British Empire*, 36
18 W. Raleigh, *History of the World*, I.VIII.i; vi.

19 Quoted in P. Rossi, *Dark Abyss of Time*, 219, from J. Woodward, *Remarks upon the Antient and Present State of London...*, London 1723, 25–6, 32.
20 J. Aubrey, *Wiltshire Collections* (Bodl.MS Aubrey 3), 1659, quoted by A. Powell (ed), *Brief Lives and other selected writings by John Aubrey*, London 1949, 1–2; S. Piggott, *Ruins*, 8–9.
21 Quoted by Keith Thomas, *Man and the Natural World*, 131.
22 A. Sammes, *Britannia Antiqua Illustrata*, 74–98; 119–24; S. Piggott, *The Earliest Wheeled Transport*, London & New York 1983, 229–35.
23 J. Hornell, *British Coracles and Irish Curraghs* (Soc, Nautical Research), London 1958; cf. P. Johnstone, *Antiq.* XXXVI, 1962, 32; XXXVIII, 1964, 284.
24 A. Marvell, *Upon Appleton House* (written *c*.1652–53).
25 W. Raleigh, *History of the World*, I.VIII.iii; X.7.
26 H. Rowlands, *Mona Antiqua Restaurata*, Dublin 1723, 23.
27 S.R. Meyrick & C.H. Smith, *The Costume of the Original Inhabitants of the British Islands ...*, London 1815.
28 For the distinction between ethnography and anthropology in this context, B. Orme, *Anthropology for Archaeologists*, London 1981.
29 M. Hodgen, *Early Anthropology in the Sixteenth and Seventeenth Centuries*, Philadelphia 1964, 111–12; S. Piggott, *Ruins*, 25–32; M. Balfour, *Edmund Harman*, Burford (Tolsey Museum), 1988.
30 P. Hulton, *America 1585: the complete drawings of John White*, Univ. N.Carolina Press & British Museum 1984, 28–30; K. Birket-Smith, *Folk*, I, 1959, 5–14; F. Yates, *The Valois Tapestries*, Warburg Inst. Studies, London 1959, 20; I. Whitaker, *Antiq.* LI 1977, 44 (kayaks); J. Bakker, *Antiq.* LIII, 107.
31 Quoted by H. Trevor-Roper, *Renaissance Essays*, London 1985, 140.
32 P. Hulton, *America 1585*, passim.
33 T.D. Kendrick, *British Antiquity*, 124, Pl.XIIIb (London MS); S. Piggott, *The*

Druids, 1975, Fig.85 (Ghent MS), J.A. Bakker, *Antiq.* LIII, 1979, 107 (Stonehenge).

34 M. Hodgen, *Early Anthropology*, 176 (costume books); F. Yates, *Valois Tapestries*.

35 D.B. Quinn, *The Elizabethans and the Irish*, Cornell 1966, 93–6 with Pls. 3–5.

36 T.D. Kendrick, *British Antiquity*, 123–5 with Pls. XIII–XVI; P. Hulton, *America 1585*, 17–18, 185, 191–2 with Pls.65–9, Figs. 28–33.

37 S. Piggott, *Ruins*, 10.

38 A.V.B. Norman, *Proc. Soc. Ant. Scot.* 116, 1986, 581; and Dr Norman *in litt.* August 1988.

39 M. Macgregor, *Early Celtic Art in North Britain*, Leicester 1976, 85–6; S. Piggott, *Ruins*, 10.

40 B. Orme, *Anthropology for Archaeologists*, 7, Figs. 6, 7.

41 M. McKisack, *Rev. Eng. Studies* XXIII, 1947, 226–43; T.D. Kendrick, *British Antiquity*, 110.

42 *Anatomy of Melancholy*, 2:2:4, 'To the Reader'.

43 *Geography Delineated*, 1625, quoted by M. Hodgen, *Early Anthropology*, 344.

44 *Leviathan*, Chap. 13.

45 W. Dugdale, *Antiquities of Warwickshire*, 1656, 788.

46 R. Plot, *Natural History of Staffordshire*, 1686, 397.

47 R.T. Gunther, *Life and Letters of Edward Lhwyd*, 425. The letter was published in *Phil. Trans.* no.337, 1713, 97.

48 J. Hawkesworth, *An Account of the Voyages ... in the southern Hemisphere*, 1773; B. Smith, *European Vision and the South Pacific 1768–1850*, Oxford 1960, Pbk. 1969, 24.

49 S. Johnson, *A Journey to the Western Islands...*, 1775, 141.

CHAPTER 4 [pp.87–122]

1 G. Clark, 'The Invasion Hypothesis in British Archaeology', *Antiq.* XL, 1966, 172.

2 M.J.S. Rudwick, *The Meaning of Fossils*, London & New York 1972.

3 O. Impey & A. Macgregor (eds) *The Origins of Museums*, Oxford 1985.

4 S. Piggott, *Ruins*, 108–09.

5 S. Piggott, *Ruins*, 135–9.

6 R.T. Gunther (ed) *Life & Letters of Edward Lhwyd*, Oxford 1945, 418–25.

7 G.F. Black, *Proc. Soc. Antiq. Scot.* XXVI, 1892–3, 433, esp. 462–8.

8 Ed. S. Sanderson, Folklore Soc. London 1976.

9 *Auctarium musei Balfouriani e musaeo Sibbaldiano*, Edinburgh 1697.

10 *Remarks and Collections of Thomas Hearne*, Oxford Hist. Soc. Oxford, VII, 1886, entries of Oct. 7 1707 and Nov. 22 1708.

11 R.T. Gunther, *Early Science in Oxford* III, Oxford 1925, 237, 336.

12 S. Piggott, 'Bronze, Britons and Romans' in R. Miket and C. Burgess (eds) *Between and Beyond the Walls: Essays ... in honour of George Jobey*, Edinburgh 1984, 117–25.

13 Conveniently accessible in Gwyn Walters (ed.), *Camden's Wales*.

14 T. Hearne in appendices of his *Itinerary of John Leland*, Oxford 1711, I, IV.

15 Quoted by D. Douglas, *English Scholars*, 68.

16 Cf. M. Todd, *The Northern Barbarians*, Oxford 1987.

17 Aubrey in *Brief Lives* (ed. A. Powell) 1949, 15; Stukeley, S. Piggott *William Stukeley*, 28.

18 Quoted by M. 'Espinasse in C. Webster (ed.) *Intellectual Revolution*, 349n.

19 C. Chippindale, *Stonehenge Complete*, London & New York 1983, is an invaluable survey of the history of the monument from medieval to modern times; G. Lambrick, *The Rollright Stones*, London 1988, 5.

20 J.A. Bakker, *Antiq.* LIII, 1979, 107, Pl.X.

21 The MS was printed by Thomas Hearne at the end of his edition of *Langtoft's Chronicle*, 1725. The authorship has been assigned to John Gibbons (1629–1718) but a case has recently been

made for Robert Gay, Rector of Nettlecombe, Somerset, 1631–72. (R. Legg, *Stonehenge Antiquaries*, Milborne Port, 1986.)

22 [E. Bolton] *Nero Caesar or Monarchie depraved*, 1614, 181, Cf. S. Piggott, *William Stukeley*, 86.

23 Inigo Jones (ed. John Webb) *The most notable Antiquity of Great Britain, vulgarly called STONE-HENG on Salisbury Plain ...* London 1655; reprinted (with Charleton & Webb), London 1725.

24 Walter Charleton, *Chorea Gigantum, or the most famous Antiquity of Great Britain, vulgarly called STONE-HENG standing on Salisbury Plain, Restored to the DANES*, London 1662.

25 For Ole Worm (1588–1654), O. Klindt-Jensen, *A History of Scandinavian Archaeology*, London & New York 1975, 18–24.

26 John Webb, *A Vindication of Stone-Heng restored ...*, London 1664.

27 A. Powell, *John Aubrey and his Friends*, 60, 105–7.

28 S. Piggott, *Ruins*, 46–47.

29 The lavish publication, *John Aubrey: Monumenta Britannica* (eds. J. Fowles & R. Legg, Milborne Port, Vol.I 1980; Vol.II 1982) is unfortunately not a scholarly edition: the transcription and editing are amateurish, inaccurate and inadequate. The facsimiles are useful but lack the folio numbering of the original, Bodleian MSS Top. Gen. c.24, 25.

30 G. Walters & F. Emery, 'Edward Lhuyd, Edmund Gibson and the printing of Camden's *Britannia*, 1695', *The Library* 5th S. XXXII, 1977, 109–37.

31 C.A. Gordon, 'Professor James Garden's letters to John Aubrey 1692–1695', *Third Spalding Club Miscellany* III, 1960.

32 R.T. Gunther, *Life and Letters of Edward Lhwyd*, 421.

33 M.J. O'Kelly, *Newgrange*, London & New York 1982.

34 S. Piggott, "Vast Perennial Memorials': the first antiquaries look at Megaliths', in J.D. Evans *et al* (eds), *Antiquity and Man*, London & New York 1981, 19–25.

35 S. Piggott *Ruins*, 109; *Antiquity Depicted*, 42.

36 S. Piggott, *Ruins*, 13–14 quoting *Oglander Memoirs 1595–1648*, 1888, 117.

37 Cf. S. Piggott, *Ruins*, 14; *Oxford Journ. Arch.* 7. 1988. 257.269 (Browne).

38 D. Douglas, *English Scholars*, 200.

CHAPTER 5 [pp. 123–59]

1 Cf.S. Piggott, *Ruins*, 55–76.

2 G.R. Cragg, *The Church and the Age of Reason 1648–1789*, Pelican History of the Church, Harmondsworth 1970; B. Willey, *Seventeenth Century* and *Eighteenth Century Background*.

3 S. Piggott, *William Stukeley*; Antiq. LX, 1986, 115–22 for references unless cited separately.

4 E. Moir, *The Discovery of Britain: The English Tourists 1540–1840*, London 1964; S. Piggott, *Ruins*, 122–7.

5 It may be represented by British Library MSS Sloane 1023, 1024; cf. S. Piggott, *Ruins*, 18; *Antiquity Depicted*, 42.

6 S. Piggott, *Ruins*, 55–76.

7 Bodleian Library MS Eng. misc. c.323; Cardiff Public Library MS 4.253.

8 Bodleian Library MS Gough Maps 231. ff. 43, 233. Reproduced by J. Thurnam, *Arch.* XLII, 1869, 161–44.

9 D.F. Allen, *The Coins of the Ancient Celts*, Edinburgh 1980, 2; D. Nash, *Coinage in the Celtic World*, London 1987.

10 D.F. Allen, *Numis. Chron.* 7s X, 1970, 117–32.

11 Cardiff Pub. Library MS 2.371, ff. 5/6.

12 S. Piggott, *Ruins*, 117; M. 'Espinasse, 'The Decline and Fall of Restoration Science', in C. Webster (ed) *Intellectual Revolution*, 347–68.

13 S. Gibson, *Oxoniensia* I, 1936, 173–95, S. Piggott, 'Antiquarian Studies', in L.S. Sutherland & L.G. Mitchell (eds), *Hist. Univ. Oxford: the Eighteenth Century* Oxford 1986, 757–77. D. Woolner, *Folklore*, 78, 1967, 90; J.V.S. Megaw, *Art of European Iron Age*, Bath 1970, 118 (White Horse).

14 T.D. Kendrick, *The Druids*, London 1927; S. Piggott, *The Druids*, London & New York 1975; A.L. Owen, *The Famous Druids*, Oxford 1962; S. Piggott, *Ruins*, 70–3; *William Stukeley*, 79–109; C. Chippindale, *Stonehenge Complete*. J. Michell, *Megalithomania*, London & New York 1982 is quite unscholarly but has good illustrations.

15 S.H. Daniel, *John Toland: his methods manners and mind*, Kingston & Montreal 1984, a study which however ignores Toland's work on the Druids.

16 *A Collection of Several Pieces of Mr John Toland*, ed. P. Desmaiseaux, London, 2 vols 1726; the *History of the Druids* is in vol. I, 1–238.

17 W.J. Harrison, 'A Bibliography of ... Stonehenge and Avebury', in *Wilts. Arch. Mag.* XXXII, 1901, 141.

18 British Library, MSS Harleian 7354, 7355.

19 For Wood, J. Summerson, 'John Wood and English Town Planning', in *Heavenly Mansions*, London 1949, New York 1963, 87–110; H.M. Colvin *Biographical Dictionary of British Architects 1600–1840*, London 1978, 908–12; S. Piggott, *The Druids* 143–6. Quotations from *Choir Gawre...* , Oxford 1747.

20 R. G. Collingwood & J.N.L. Myres, *Roman Britain and the English Settlements*, Oxford 1936, 250.

21 Cf. R.F. Jones *et al*, *The Seventeenth Century*, Stanford Univ. Press 1951, 10–74.

22 J.M. Levine, *Dr Woodward's Shield*, Univ. California Press 1977, 240.

23 J. Seznec, *Essais sur Diderot et l' Antiquité*, Oxford 1957, esp. Chap. V, 'Le Singe Antiquaire'.

24 L. Whitney, *Mod. Philology* XXI, 1924, 337; A.O. Lovejoy, *Essays in the History of Ideas* no.II; S. Piggott, *Ruins*, 151–4.

25 B. Orme, *Antiq.* XLVIII, 1974, 116; Joan Evans, *Hist. Soc. Antiqs.* 153.

26 John Evans, *Ancient Stone Implements...* London 1872; *Ancient Bronze Implements* ... London 1881; J. Thurnam, *Arch.* XLII, 1869, 161–244; XLIII, 1873, 285–544.

27 L.V. Grinsell, *Folklore*, 78, 1967, 1–38.

28 P. Ashbee, *Bronze Age Round Barrow in Britain*, London 1960, 19, makes the count 379; B.M. Marsden, *The Early Barrow-Diggers*, Princes Risborough 1974, 118, reckons 465.

29 R.H. Cunnington, *From Antiquary to Archaeologist*, Princes Risborough 1975; K. Woodbridge *Landscape and Antiquity*, Oxford 1970, for all quotations.

30 Illustrated by Hoare in *Tumuli Wiltunenses*, Shaftesbury 1829, 8.

31 C.A. Stothard, *Memoirs...* , London 1823, 74.

32 Cf.S. Piggott, *Antiquity Depicted*, 7.

33 B.M. Marsden, *The Early Barrow-Diggers*, with quotations.

34 G. Daniel, *The Origins and Growth of Archaeology*, Harmondsworth 1967, 57–78 with quotations.

Further reading

The notes to the text give the documentation for specific points, but from these a selection of sources may be chosen for readers who wish to explore the background further.

In general we may start with Basil Willey, *The Seventeenth Century Background* (London 1934) and *The Eighteenth Century Background* (London 1940) from the literary viewpoint; Hugh Trevor-Roper, *Renaissance Essays* (London 1985) and *Catholics, Anglicans and Puritans* (London 1987) for individuals in their political setting (Camden, Stow, Burton, Ussher); Charles Webster, *The Great Instauration* (London 1975) for the early scientific background, and David Douglas, *English Scholars* (London 1939) for the historians.

The more directly antiquarian aspects are contained in Michael Hunter, *John Aubrey and the Realm of Learning* (London 1975) and *Science and Society in Restoration England* (Cambridge 1981); Stuart Piggott, *Ruins in a Landscape* (Edinburgh 1976); *Antiquity Depicted* (London & New York 1978); Joan Evans,

A History of the Society of Antiquaries (Oxford 1956).

For the Renaissance antiquaries, T.D. Kendrick, *British Antiquity* (London 1950) with J.M. Levine, *Humanism and History* (Cornell 1987), and for ethnographical parallels M.T. Hodgen, *Early Anthropology in the Sixteenth and Seventeenth Centuries* (Univ. Pennsylvania 1964). The problems of chronology and the Old Testament are discussed in P. Rossi, *The Dark Abyss of Time* (Chicago & London 1984); D.C. Allen, *The Legend of Noah* (Urbana 1949); R.H. Popkin, *Isaac Lapeyrère* (Leiden & New York 1987); E. Iversen, *The Myth of Egypt and its Hieroglyphics* (Copenhagen 1961). The eighteenth-century antiquarian scene is surveyed in J.M. Levine, *Dr Woodward's Shield* (Univ. California 1977); Stuart Piggott, *William Stukeley* (London & New York 1985); *The Druids* (London & New York 1975); and its close in K. Woodbridge, *Landscape and Antiquity* (Oxford 1970); B. Marsden, *The Early Barrow-Diggers* (Princes Risborough 1974).

List of illustrations

TEXT FIGURES

1 Ancient Dutch giants and the megalithic tomb they have built, engraving from Johan Picardt, *Korte Beschryvinghe van eenige Vergetene en Vorbegene Antiquiteten* (1660).

2 Third title-page to Theodor De Bry, *America* (1950).

3 'A man of nation neighbour vnto the Picte', from Theodor De Bry, *America* (1590).

4 'A woman nighbour to the Pictes', from Theodor De Bry, *America* (1590).

5 Ancient British woman from John Speed, *The Historie of Great Britaine* (1611).

6 Ancient British man from John Speed, *The Historie of Great Britaine* (1611).

7 Detail of engraved title-page, from John Speed, *Theatre of the Empire of Great Britaine* (1611).

8 Boadicea reviewing her troops, from Raphael Holinshed's *Chronicles* (1578).

9 Staffordshire antiquities, from Robert Plot, *The Natural History of Stafford-shire* (1686).

10 Scottish antiquities, engraving from Sir Robert Sibbald's *Miscellanea quaedam eruditae antiquitatis* (1710).

11 Scottish antiquities, engraving from Sir Robert Sibbald's *Miscellanea quaedam eruditae antiquitatis* (1710).

12 Plan of the hillfort of Y Dinas, Llanwnda, Pembrokeshire, by William Jones for Edward Lhuyd, 1697–8. British Museum, Stowe MS 1024 f. 43.

13 Standing stones known as The Devil's Arrows, Boroughbridge, West Yorkshire. Engraving from Thomas Gale, *Antonini Iter Britanniarum*, edited by his son Roger (1709).

14 Title–page drawn by William Stukeley for unpublished book on Avebury and Stonehenge. Bodleian Library, Oxford, MS Eng Misc 323 f.1r.

15 Stukeley's drawings of 'Enginry' for *Stonehenge*. Cardiff City Library, MS.4. 253 ff. 125, 126.

16 Engraving of Cornish Stone Circles, from a drawing by William Borlase, *Antiquities ... of the County of Cornwall* (1754).

17 Bookplate of Clerk of Penicuik, early nineteenth century. Collection Sir John Clerk.

PLATES

1 William Camden (1551–1623), portrait medallion, c.1623. Bronze, diameter approx. 40 mm. British Museum, London.

2 John Aubrey (1626–97), engraving after a drawing by William Faithorne the Elder, 1660, from J. Britton, *Memoir of John Aubrey* (1845).

3 Robert Plot (1640–96), oil painting by an unknown artist.

Index

Bold numerals refer to text figures; *italic* numerals indicate plates

Index